Fi... ,
My Brethren

rethinking
spiritual warfare

Revised and Enlarged
2013

By Dr. Delron Shirley

In loving memory of my mother
Hattie Ruth Timms Shirley
1922-2003

This teaching manual is intended for personal study; however, the author encourages all students to also become teachers and to share the truths from this text with others. However, copying the text itself without permission from the author is considered plagiarism, which is punishable by law. To obtain permission to quote material from this book, please contact:

Table of Contents

Don't Begin at the End 1

Faithfulness 3

Knowing Our Position 9

Blameless and Curseless 12

Predestined for Victory 15

Tamperproof 22

Supernatural Wisdom and Revelation 24

Our Transformation from the Kingdom of Darkness 28

Our Position in the Body of Christ 36

Realizing the New Creation Within Us 46

Radically Different from Our Old Unregenerate Man 50

Walking Circumspectly 53

Knowing the Will of God 58

Offensive Movement 62

Submission 73

After Having Eaten The Baby 81

The Grammar 82

Standing vs. Wrestling 84

Pulling Down Strongholds 93

Becoming a Prayer Warrior 98

Knowing Our Enemy 102

Picking Our Battleground 105

Choosing Our Weapons 109

And the Winner is 113

What the Devil? 115

Where Did the Devil Come From? 130

Power, Might, and Dominion 138

Christians and Demons 153

Destroying the Works of the Devil 170

The Violent Take the Kingdom by Force 184

A Snake in the Grass -- or At Least in the Tree 198

Epilogue 199

Don't Begin at the End

I have been to so many seminars and attended so many services on the topic of spiritual warfare that my Bible almost jumps open to Ephesians chapter six verse ten on its own. It seems that everyone who teaches on the topic starts with this classic verse. "Finally, my brethren, be strong in the Lord and in the power of his might." (Ephesians 6:10) However, the word "finally" should be a clue to us that there is really another place we should be starting. In the same way that we don't read a book from the last chapter and we don't climb a ladder from the top rung, we can't start our spiritual warfare at the final point. The word "finally" means "in conclusion" or "bringing a summary to what has previously been said, we come to a concluding point." With this in mind, we must see Ephesians 6:10 as the ending, not the starting point, in understanding spiritual warfare.

Out of all the messages we have heard on spiritual warfare, we have probably never heard anyone lay a groundwork for the word "finally" in chapter six verse ten. Speakers usually just jump into the passage without looking back to what Paul has previously said. Yet, if we are going to have a real understanding of where we will end up finally, we have to look back to see the whole journey which has brought us to this final point. There are five and a half absolutely indispensable chapters that precede Ephesians 6:10. We must have this knowledge and foundation incorporated into our lives before we are able to grasp the true meaning and power of Ephesians 6:10.

By starting at the end rather than the beginning in their study of spiritual warfare, many Christians have entered into spiritual warfare ill prepared, only to come back bruised and bleeding. They went out with the "finally, my brethren" challenge, but lacked the preparation it takes to get to this final stage. When the devil is able to inflict this sort of collateral damage on the Body of Christ, he has triumphed in his strategy because he has not only wounded one soldier but has also pulled other good warriors from the frontlines to tend to their fallen comrade and has discouraged even more recruits from joining in the fight at all.

There are many layers of what we might call "underwear" that we have to put on before we can don the spiritual armor. Paul has taken the entire book of Ephesians to lay the groundwork to get us to the point where we are able to put on this final warfare armament. We often think of Christians as arrayed in the shining armor of a medieval knight going into battle. But I -- for one -- would not want to wear all that metal outerwear without the proper padding underneath. The same is true with our spiritual armor.

Before Paul teaches us about the spiritual armor, he helps us develop our spiritual authority because he knows that unless there is a warrior inside of us there won't be a warrior inside our uniforms. In fact, even when he makes his classic statement in this touchstone verse on spiritual warfare, his direction is actually focused on who we are more than what we put on. He directs us to be strong; putting on the external armor seems almost secondary to this commandment to exert our internal strength. You see, God is not in the business of just passing out uniforms; He is in the business of equipping soldiers. Remember -- if there's not a warrior inside of you, there won't be one inside your uniform!

Faithfulness

Paul opens his letter to the Ephesians by addressing them as saints and as faithful. It would seem obvious that it is saints -- not sinners -- who are going to be waging spiritual warfare against the devil. After all, why would anyone who is still on Satan's team try to fight against him? The second quality he mentions is the concept of faithfulness that has been woefully lacking in most contemporary Christian teaching -- yet it is a vital key to spiritual victory.

We are all desirous of being overcomers and more than conquerors. Unfortunately we too often feel that we can achieve these spiritual qualities through some "spiritual microwave" quick fix, such as having some anointed spiritual leader lay hands on us or by going on an extended fast. We seem to have forgotten (or maybe never learned) that in order to overcome, we must endure -- all the way to the end. In describing the Christian life we are called to, Jesus said, "And ye shall be hated of all men for my name's sake: but he that endureth to the end shall be saved." (Matthew 10:22) The quality that keeps us on task to the point that we can be said to be enduring and eventually overcoming is called faithfulness.

When St. John was given a vision of the victorious army of the redeemed (overcomers at their best) returning with Christ for history's final conquest of evil (the ultimate in spiritual warfare), he listed only three qualifying requirements. While two of these qualifiers are totally at God's own discretion, one is under the control of the individual. The only character trait listed that the individual Christian can develop in order to be numbered among the overcomers is faithfulness!

> These (Antichrist's forces) shall make war with the Lamb, and the Lamb shall overcome them: for he is Lord of lords, and King of kings: and they that are with him are called, and chosen, and faithful.

(Revelation 17:14)

If each individual soldier is not faithful to appear at all the roll calls, practice all the drills, and follow all the commands of his superior officers, there is no army. Just as no army can exist if the soldiers are unfaithful and undependable, the spiritual army of God cannot be successful in its mission unless each of its members develops faithfulness.

The world is full of Christians who began the race but eventually dropped out. Because they could not stay on focus, they lacked the staying power necessary to succeed. Because faithfulness is a major attribute that equips an individual for the "long haul," it is one of the main qualities God is looking for -- and requiring -- in His servants. "Moreover it is required in stewards, that a man be found faithful." (I Corinthians 4:2)

Psalm 101:4-8 contrasts God's pleasure with the faithful and His contempt for those who lack this quality.

A froward heart shall depart from me: I will not know a wicked person. Whoso privily slandereth his neighbour, him will I cut off: him that hath an high look and a proud heart will not I suffer. Mine eyes shall be upon the faithful of the land, that they may dwell with me: he that walketh in a perfect way, he shall serve me. He that worketh deceit shall not dwell within my house: he that telleth lies shall not tarry in my sight. I will early destroy all the wicked of the land; that I may cut off all wicked doers from the city of the LORD.

Notice all the contrasting options this passage offers when listing those who lack faithfulness: the forward (or perverse) of heart, the wicked persons, those who slander their neighbors, ones with high looks and proud hearts, those who work deceit, and those who tell lies. Not only do these who fail to qualify as the faithful lack the admirable quality of being able to stick to the task, they actually display a long list of negative and destructive attributes. There is no middle ground where we can be good guys in every area except that we are just a little short on our loyalty. Notice how Jesus described the person who lacked faithfulness:

> And the Lord said, Who then is that faithful and wise steward, whom his lord shall make ruler over his household, to give them their portion of meat in due season? Blessed is that servant, whom his lord when he cometh shall find so doing. Of a truth I say unto you, that he will make him ruler over all that he hath. But and if that servant say in his heart, My lord delayeth his coming; and shall begin to beat the menservants and maidens, and to eat and drink, and to be drunken; The lord of that servant will come in a day when he looketh not for him, and at an hour when he is not aware, and will cut him in sunder, and will appoint him his portion with the unbelievers. And that servant, which knew his lord's will, and prepared not himself, neither did according to his will, shall be beaten with many stripes. (Luke 12:42-47)

As soon as the servant of the Lord abandons faithfulness, he becomes abusive (beating the other servants), self-indulgent (eating and drinking to excess), negligent concerning his responsibilities (not looking for the master to whom he is responsible), faithless (he is listed among the unbelieving), rebellious (knowing his lord's will but not doing it), and careless about his faith (being unprepared for the return of his lord). Who would have thought that so much depended upon our being faithful? Normally, we think that there are only temporary and immediate short-ranged consequences if we let our responsibilities slide. We think that our actions are either of no consequence at all or that they will produce only a small ripple effect.

For example, we know that we should be faithful in our tithing, but we feel that there will not be any really big consequences if we fudge a bit one week. We may think, "Sure, the church will be out a few dollars; but what does that matter? Everyone else is giving, and there may even be a visitor who will drop a little something extra into the offering plate. Besides, what does my offering have to do with the total budget of the church anyway?" The thing we fail to recognize is that when we hold back on our tithing we are actually inviting the devourer into our lives. In Malachi 3:11, God obligated Himself to the task of rebuking the devourer away from the lives those who tithe. As soon as we fail in our faithfulness to this responsibility, God's "hands are tied" so that He can no longer resist the devil for us. When the devourer rushes in, he will certainly begin to eat up our finances, but do you think he'll stop there? Of course not, he will eat up any and everything he can get to: our health, or relationships, and -- as we can tell from the parable we just read -- our character!

While practicing faithfulness in small matters will help us to develop a greater sense of responsibility, unfaithfulness concerning even the slightest of our obligations will lead us to shirk more important responsibilities. Jesus said, "He that is faithful in that which is least is faithful also in much: and he that is unjust in the least is unjust also in much." (Luke 16:10) Failing in our faithfulness has more than just a simple ripple effect. A more accurate illustration could be drawn from a little story we learned at our mothers' knees about the little Dutch boy who held his finger in the dike to keep the city from flooding. The breach in our faithfulness may look like a tiny hole, but it will soon make the whole dam collapse and we will be inundated!

While we are busily pursuing more flashy spiritual manifestations, it may be very easy to overlook the "wallflower" quality of faithfulness. According to Proverbs 20:6, "Most men will proclaim every one his own goodness: but a faithful man who can find? " The average man is busy "putting on airs" trying to make himself look good and cover up the fact that he has a perverse heart, is wicked, slanders his neighbor, is proud, works deceit, and tells lies; all the while the faithful man lives a simple, unassuming life which may make him almost melt into the background. He may not stand out as a superstar to men, but -- and this is an all-important "but" -- he will attract the attention of God.

When we have God's attention, we become targets for His blessings. In His parables, Jesus repeatedly spoke of the promotion that the Lord has in store for those He considers to be faithful.

> His lord said unto him, Well done, good and faithful servant; thou hast been faithful over a few things, I will make thee ruler over many things: enter thou into the joy of thy lord. (Matthew 25:23)
> And the Lord said, Who then is that faithful and wise steward, whom his lord shall make ruler over his household, to give them their portion of meat in due season? (Luke 12:42)

Advancement, finances, and spiritual fulfillment are the inheritance of those who are deemed faithful and dependable. God rewards faithfulness because it shows stability. Because He knows that a faithful person is trustworthy, He will entrust him with gifts, privileges, and responsibilities. He knows that the faithful person will be with Him when He needs him and that he will take on any responsibility with the same care he has consistently shown.

At the literal conclusion of spiritual warfare as the final blows are being struck at the Valley of Megiddo, even Jesus Christ Himself will be identified with two outstanding qualities -- one being His faithfulness! "And I saw heaven opened, and behold a white horse; and he that sat upon him was called Faithful and True, and in righteousness he doth judge and make war." (Revelation 19:11)

Knowing Our Position

Paul then turns to the topic of knowing our relationship with God. It is a necessity for us to know our position with Christ in God before we go out to fight the enemy.

> Blessed be the God and Father of our Lord Jesus Christ, who hath blessed us with all spiritual blessings in heavenly places in Christ. (verse 1:3)

We are not just blessed with some spiritual blessings, but we are blessed with all spiritual blessings. The first thing we have to realize about this passage is that it is written to all believers, not some elite group of church leaders. It is all too easy for us to begin to think that pastors and televangelists have some extra spiritual blessings that we as laymen lack. On the contrary, Paul described the entire church as having all spiritual blessings.

In a later passage (verse 2:6), Paul told us that we are seated with Christ in heavenly places, far above every principality and power. It is important for us to recognize that we are seated with Christ and that we are blessed with every spiritual blessing in Christ. If we are with Christ and in Christ in those heavenly places, then we are seated together with Christ and hold a position far above every principality and every power.

Most people, when trying to enter into an understanding of spiritual warfare, neglect this basic foundational truth. They enter into the study thinking that they are nose to nose with the devil, on equal ground with him, and that it is up to them to somehow outfox and outwrestle him. But Paul does not take us into spiritual warfare with the understanding that we have a fifty-fifty chance of winning or losing because we are on equal ground with the enemy. Paul went into the teaching on spiritual warfare building on one basic foundation: "I am with Christ, and I am seated with Christ in heavenly places far above all principalities and powers." If we go into spiritual warfare with the knowledge that we have the upper hand from the beginning, an entirely new revelation of spiritual warfare opens up to us. We generally think of spiritual warfare as quickly fighting back before the devil throws another punch. Paul did not depict spiritual warfare as being out of fear or intimidation; rather, he said that we already have the upper hand in our fight. We are already seated above principalities. They are far below us, and we have the advantage. He goes into this teaching with a positive victor's attitude.

It, of course, helps if we understand how battles were fought in biblical days. Today, we have an entirely different perspective on warfare because we use modern ballistic armaments. At the time of Paul's writing, warfare was hand-to-hand combat. If you happened to be on higher ground, you had a definite advantage over your enemy on lower ground because gravity was working with you. When you threw your spear, it was propelled by not only your energy but also by the force of gravity. Gravitational force actually accelerated your spear at a rate of thirty-two feet per second -- and that was to the second power! Your enemy was at a disadvantage because he had to exert most of his energy to overcome gravity to be able to throw his spear toward you. As he was throwing his spear up, gravity was trying to pull it back down. The force of gravity pulling it down would cause the spear to virtually stop in midair and fall to the ground. Gravity would actually negate all the energy that your enemy had put into the battle. In fact, their weapons could actually fall back upon them! Remember the story told in the book of Esther of how Haman wound up being hanged from the gallows he had constructed for Mordecai (Esther 9:25) and the adage in Psalm 7:15 that your enemy might dig a ditch to entrap you but would wind up falling into it himself!

Paul said that we are seated in heavenly places. We are blessed with all spiritual blessings because we are seated higher than the demon forces. Spiritual gravity is on our side. Our spear, with our force complemented by spiritual gravity, zeroes right in on the target. Because the devil's forces are working against the law of spiritual gravity, they are negated. Battles and attacks will continue to come, but we know from the book of Isaiah that no weapon that is formed against us will prosper. (verse 54:17) Their weapons cannot prosper because we are sitting higher than the demon forces that are attacking us.

Blameless and Curseless

Paul tells us that we are holy and without blame.

> According as he hath chosen us in him
> before the foundation of the world, that we
> should be holy and without blame before
> him in love. (verse 1:4)

When Balaam was called to put a curse on the children of Israel, he went to a high place to overlook the people encamped in the valleys before him. As he opened his mouth to hurl a curse at them, out flowed a blessing instead. He tried again and again, but every time his curses came out as blessings. After being confronted by Balak, Balaam replied, "How shall I curse, whom God hath not cursed? or how shall I defy, whom the LORD hath not defied?" (Numbers 23:8) The book of Revelation tells us that the sin of Balaam was that he taught Israel to commit adultery and to eat meat sacrificed to idols. (verse 2:14) Reading between the lines, we are able to see what must have transpired between the prophet and the king: Balaam told Balak, "If the children of Israel curse themselves by breaking the Ten Commandments that the Lord has just given them, then I won't need to curse them. If God curses them because of their disobedience, then you won't need my assistance." The next chapter in Numbers tells us that the people of Israel did indeed commit adultery with the women of Balak's tribe and that those women led them into idolatry and eating meat sacrificed to idols. Balaam could not overcome the spiritual force of God's blessings upon the people, so he devised a plan to cause the people of Israel to walk out from under God's blessing. Deuteronomy chapter twenty-eight tells us that if we keep all the commandments of God, we will be blessed coming in and going out. However, those who do not keep the commandments of God are cursed coming in and going out.

God has chosen us to be "holy and without blame before him in love." (verse 1:4) If we are holy and without blame, we will live in the blessings of God and cannot be cursed. It doesn't matter how many demons might come against us with all their wiles; their curses will bounce off because they cannot curse whom God has not cursed. It didn't work for Balaam, and it won't work for any devil today. In Proverbs 26:2, the wise man Solomon said that it is no more likely for a curse without a cause to come into our lives than it is for wild birds to land on our shoulders. However, if we are in disobedience to God and He has given us over to be cursed, then their curses can take hold. If we align with His choice that we would be holy and without blame before Him in love, then He will set up the conditions that will put us in the place where no curse will ever be able to attach itself to us. On the other hand, it can be totally devastating for us to try to enter into spiritual warfare if we are not in the right relationship with God -- holy and without blame. Our enemy is the accuser of the brethren (Revelation 12:10), and he will try to slander us before God just as he did Job; however, our God will defend us just as He did this ancient saint. (Job 1:8) The other wonderful promise we have is that we have a ready remedy if our lives are not blameless: "If we confess our sins, he is faithful and just to forgive us our sins, and to cleanse us from all unrighteousness." (I John 1:9)

Deuteronomy 23:14 teaches us, "The Lord your God moves about in your camp to protect you and to deliver your enemies to you. Your camp must be holy, so that He will not see among you anything indecent and turn away from you." If we are anticipating to win spiritual victories, we must start with allowing God to make us victorious within our own personal lives.

In my years of experience teaching in Bible colleges, I've had some very interesting students -- some of which came from backgrounds in the occult. One young man was a high priest in a Satanic cult before he was born again, and one young lady was a practicing witch before her conversion. Both of these students told some fascinating stories which confirmed the principles Paul presented here.

Jeff related his experience of "toying" with his demonic power while standing in a second story window, watching the people on the sidewalk below. On snowy days, he would command people to slip on the icy pavement. He said that he would stand there for hours and watch the people as, one after another, they would slip and fall -- that is, most of the passersby. Occasionally there were ones who kept walking at their normal pace regardless of how much spiritual power he would exert in his attempt to make them fall. When he could identify who these individuals were, he would always find that they were born-again Christians who were really living their faith, not just wearing the label. Penny related similar stories from her days in witchcraft. She said that she eventually learned not to try to place curses on certain people because the things that she tried to impose on these targets would bounce back and attack her -- usually with worse results than what she had intended toward her victims. Again, when she was able to identify these individuals, she would discover that they were Bible-believing, Spirit-filled Christians.

Predestined for Victory

The next concept Paul introduced is that we are predestined unto the adoption of sons.

> Having predestinated us unto the adoption of children by Jesus Christ to himself, according to the good pleasure of his will.
> (verse 1:5)

Imagine the pride of the father of a newborn son. The young man holds the baby for the very first time and, looking into his firstborn's wrinkled little face, proclaims, "Son, I believe that you are really going to make a mark in this world. I expect you to succeed and someday actually be listed among the top ten on the FBI's most wanted list!" Of course not! Instead, we always pronounce high anticipation of good achievements over our children. Then we actually start putting things in motion to make our proclamation possible. We open a college fund to provide for the child's education, we make regular appointments with the pediatrician to ensure that the child's body is properly cared for, and -- interestingly enough -- studies show that we actually start attending church more regularly to guarantee that our child's spiritual life is secure. If we as humans have that instinct, certainly God would never proclaim evil destinies over His creation. If we look at all the passages concerning God's foreknowledge and predestation, we will find that every one of them is in the context of His anticipation that we will succeed. There is never a hint that He purposely or randomly predestined some to be saved and blessed and others to be lost and damned -- as some people teach when considering the doctrines of predestation and God's sovereignty. Ephesians 1:5, for example, says that He has predestinated us unto the adoption of children according to the <u>good pleasure</u> of <u>his will</u> -- which isn't to be on the FBI's Ten Most Wanted List! For further study, please read Jeremiah 29:11, John 3:16-18, Acts 2:23, Romans 9:1-33, Romans 11:2, Ephesians 1:3-14, I Peter 1:2, and II Peter 3:9.

Predestination is a doctrine that is often misunderstood. Some have the concept that there are those who are predestined beforehand to be good and that others are predestined to be bad. They think that some are predestined to be saved and that others are predestined to be damned. Many people envision God's choosing: "Eeny, meeny, miney, moe. You are saved; you are damned. You are blessed; you are cursed." However, when we study all the occurrences of terms such as "predestination" or "foreknowledge," we never find that anyone is predestined to destruction. Every time predestination is mentioned, it is in a very positive light. God predestines people to be blessed, ordained, and adopted. The predestination by God is always for our blessing. God's will for mankind is that none should perish, but that all should come to repentance. There is a good pleasure to His will, and we are predestined to that. Just as no one of us would make a bad plan for the future of our children, the heavenly Father also makes good plans for the future of His children. (Jeremiah 29:11) The problem is that we don't always choose to comply with His plans.

If we walk into spiritual warfare with the revelation that God has predetermined for us to be adopted to His sonship, we have a tremendous advantage. If when we go into battle, we are not confident that God wants us to win, we can't fight with determination. God has not chosen us to be losers! He has already predetermined that He is on our side. He has chosen us on His team. He has adopted us into His sonship. He intends that we will be champions and victory trophies for Him. You might say that He intends to see our pictures on the Heavenly Wheaties box! We can go into warfare with a victor's attitude knowing that we are not losers. We must erase all the question marks in our minds and change them to explanation points. We must go into battle knowing that we will come out victoriously on the other side. No matter how many fires we have to go through, the scripture says that they won't kindle upon us.

No matter how many floods we have to walk though, we will not be drowned. (Isaiah 43:2)

After a meeting with British Prime Minister Winston Churchill to hammer out the strategy of the Anglo-American alliance for World War II, US President Franklin Roosevelt announced to the press that the two leaders were determined to accept "nothing less than unconditional surrender of Germany, Italy, and Japan!" It was this spirit that drove our men to victory, and it will be this same determination that we are nothing less than triumphant victors that will propel <u>us</u> to victory.

There is a difference between adoption and natural childbirth: the element of choice. Pregnancy is not always a conscious choice; however, adoption is never without deliberate decision. Additionally, in natural childbearing, you have to take what you get; whereas, you can set certain standards -- essentially handpicking the child -- when going through the adoption process. Wow, what a revelation -- you are not an accident but were hand picked by God!

The practice of adoption in biblical times was one of providing an avenue of passing on an inheritance. If a man had no son, he would usually adopt a nephew to become his heir. This practice kept the wealth inside the family rather than letting it be lost to outsiders. Notice in the story of Abraham and Lot it was only after Lot had separated from Abraham (Genesis 13:14) that Abraham became concerned about the fact that he had no heir (verse 15:2). Unlike adoption today, which may be based on sympathy for orphaned children or the loneliness of childless couples, the adoption mentioned here was based solely on the desire to pass on benefits. If we see our position in Christ in this light, we will understand that God is not intending that this benefit to be jeopardized in warfare. He wants to make an investment in us, and He does not intend to see that investment stolen, destroyed, or beaten up. Remember how careful you were to prevent even the slightest ding on you new car? Remember how concerned you were when your little child scraped his knee or was bullied by some kid at school? How do you think your heavenly Father will react if He sees insult or injury being inflicted upon His adopted son? One of my students told me about her concern for her son who was a fighter pilot in the Air Force. After several years of worry for his safety, she one day realized that her son had been through a multi-million-dollar training program and was flying a twenty-five-million-dollar jet. At that point, she understood that he was not in danger because the US government was not going to let such a high-dollar investment go unprotected. God has invested far more in us than the US government had invested in that you pilot.

Following immediately on the heels of this teaching, Paul said that we are accepted in the beloved.

> To the praise of the glory of his grace, wherein he hath made us accepted in the beloved. (verse 1:6)

When Paul said that we are accepted in the beloved, he used a term that appears only two times in the New Testament -- here in Ephesians 1:6 and in Luke 1:28, where the angel Gabriel used this term to tell the Virgin Mary that she was "highly favored." In other words, our acceptance is not just a toleration; it is a full-blown celebration of adoption. If we couple this understanding of the word with the context in which it is used here -- to the praise of the glory of His grace -- we will begin to get an insight into how exuberant God really is about having us as part of His family! Unlike Cinderella's stepmother, who hated and rejected her, our heavenly Father accepts and loves us.

Take a look at your refrigerator. You'll probably see so many little magnets on the door that you will begin to wonder if their magnetic force fields aren't causing a strain on the motor inside. It's likely that almost every one of those magnets is holding up a crayon drawing, a good test paper, or a photograph of your kids or grandkids. Why? Because we are proud of them and our way of letting them know it is to post their accomplishments on the refrigerator

door. Boy, I'd love to take a peek at God's refrigerator door!
I'm sure that it is loaded with trophies from every little
accomplishment by every one of His kids.

It is important for us to notice that God has made a very
costly investment in our lives. Jesus invested His very life's
blood. Certainly He is not going to leave us to protect that
kind of investment with only our own limited human ability
and intellect. He is going to actively provide for us
everything we need in order to adequately protect His
investment. There is no way that He is going to leave us
unprotected or undefended. If earthly parents -- humans
and animals -- protect their young, how much more will the
heavenly Father see to it that His sons and daughters are
under His covering when in spiritual warfare.

> In whom we have redemption through his
> blood, the forgiveness of sins, according to
> the riches of his grace. (verse 1:7)

Notice that Paul said, "according to the riches of his
grace." If we really want to get the impact of this statement,
we have to stop to understand what the word "according"
means. The connotation of this particular wording is that we
have forgiveness and redemption in direct proportion to the
riches of His grace. To visualize this better, let's stop in
front of the shopping mall on a cold wintry day just before
Christmas. Braving the bitter cold artic winds, a bell ringer
draws people's attention to the Salvation Army kettle beside
her. A gentleman, all bundled up in his warm wool topcoat,
takes a step toward her and drops something into the
collection bucket. The bell ringer smiles warmly and wishes
him a merry Christmas, never realizing that the gentleman
was a multimillionaire business tycoon and that he had just
dropped a one-dollar bill into her charity kettle. Certainly,
the gentleman had responded to the need and shown a
charitable heart. Yes, his donation would help the ministry
provide a bit of warmth to one of the homeless men who file
into their facility every day; however, his gift was not in any
way in proportion to his ability. If he had really cared to, this

one donor could have built a whole new facility for the homeless shelter and funded its operation for the whole coming year. Instead, he put in enough to provide just one cup of coffee to a needy man. Christ, on the other hand, works in our lives according -- in direct proportion -- to the riches of His grace. In other words, His provision is infinite and unlimited!

In Ephesians 1:8, Paul speaks of wisdom and prudence that He made to abound toward us. The New International Version translates this clause, "He has lavished upon us..." One fast-food restaurant puts the meat on a scale to make sure that the customer gets exactly the right number of ounces. If the scale tips a little high, the counter attendant tears off a little so that the customer gets exactly the amount he pays for -- and not a bit more. "Lavish," on the other hand, means that there is no scale. God's blessings are spread out for us like an all-you-can-eat buffet. "Lavish" actually implies an over-the-top excess -- like the world-record-breaking three-hundred-thirty-eight-pound burger produced at Mallie's Sports Grill and Bar in Southgate, Michigan; it was three feet high, had more than half a million calories, and took twenty-two hours to cook. Why did Mallie's make such a monster of a hamburger? Because they could. Why does God lavish His blessing upon us? Because He can. We serve a God named El Shaddai, the God of More Than Enough. He lavishly gives us abundance, "good measure, pressed down, and shaken together, and running over." (Luke 6:38)

Verses seven and eight list a number of things that are the result of His predestination and His self-determination: redemption through the blood, forgiveness of sins, the riches of His grace, and things that have to do with redemption, grace, and forgiveness. God knows that if He overruns our cups, we will surely have enough. We may only need a little forgiveness, but He lavishes it upon us. We may only need one dose of grace, but He lavishes it upon us. There is always more than enough. We walk into spiritual confrontation knowing that we are not just conquerors -- we are more than conquerors (Romans 8:37) because the God we serve is more than enough and He has lavished upon us all that we need for life and godliness. (II Peter 1:3)

Paul continued with "having made known to us the mystery of His will…" If we know the mystery of the will of God, we walk with a new determination. When we go into warfare, if we understand the will of God and we know how the end of the Book reads, we don't have to panic or have question marks in the middle of the struggle. Because we know that we are going to win, we can fight with renewed vigor and confidence. Ephesians 1:11 tells us that we have "obtained an inheritance, being predestinated…" We are predetermined; therefore, we know that our course has already been planned out by God and that He has a will for things to work according to His course. We must remember that inheritances go to survivors, not casualties!

Our lives are "to the praise of his glory." (verse 1:12) God is determined to make it work out that we should be to the praise of His glory. If we come out of spiritual warfare beaten, bruised, and defeated, there will be shame rather than praise for our God. Instead, we are to march out victoriously, bringing praise to God. When the three Hebrew children were thrown into the fiery furnace, they didn't come out with blisters all over them. When they came out, not even the smell of smoke was upon them, and none of the hairs on their heads had been singed. (Daniel 3:27) Their clothes were "April fresh" -- as one detergent ad would say. The only thing burned was the rope that had once held them captive. When the Babylonian king saw this victorious deliverance, he glorified the God of Israel.

Jesus Himself emphasized this same point in the Sermon on the Mount when He taught us:

> Let your light so shine before men, that they
> may see your good works, and glorify your
> Father which is in heaven. (Matthew 5:16)

Tamperproof

The little boy excitedly ripped open his package of animal crackers and very carefully began to lay them all out on the kitchen table. Suddenly, he began to cry and ran away from the table. His mother chased after him and drew his tearstained face close to her apron, asking what was the matter. Between the sobs, he blurted out that he had read the warning on the box, "Do not eat if the seal is broken." Yes, it's just a humorous little story, but the truth is that many of us are just as confused as this little boy when it comes to understanding what the seal of the Spirit really is. You see, the seal of the Spirit has to do with our protection, not salvation.

According to Ephesians 1:13, we are "sealed with that holy Spirit of promise." The Holy Spirit has put a seal, a guarantee, on us that means that we cannot be tampered with. We are tamperproof and the devil doesn't have any right to get a hold on us. Knowing this enables us to walk into spiritual battle, to take the spiritual armor and weapons, and to know that we can march toward the victory.

In 1982, seven individuals in the Chicago area died of potassium cyanide poisoning from Extra-Strength Tylenol capsules that had been tampered with after the medicine was delivered to the pharmacies in the area. These poisonings led to reforms in the packaging of over-the-counter substances and to federal anti-tampering laws. In 2003, a batch of worm-infested candy in India prompted the Cadbury Company to implement a new double-sealed wrapper for the customers' protection. Just like these products in the grocery stores and pharmacies are marked, "Do not purchase if the seal has been broken," we must ensure that the seal on our lives has not been broken. We can do this by always submitting to the conviction of the Holy Spirit when He reproves sin and error in our lives. (John 16:8) Each time we do a wrong thing, think a wrong thought, or have a wrong attitude, the Holy Spirit causes an uneasiness in our spirit man. If we will immediately acknowledge His warning and repent of that error, His seal remains intact.   If we refuse to yield to His wooing, we damage that seal and, therefore, jeopardize our purity by allowing contaminants into our spirits.   Paul frequently mentioned his good or pure conscience. (Acts 23:1, II Timothy 1:3) He knew the power of living his life free from tampering with the tamperproof seal that the Holy Spirit placed upon his heart.   I can imagine that he must have learned a lesson from the story of David's defeat of Goliath. The stone from the shepherd's sling found that singular point of vulnerability in the giant's armor -- the opening between his eyes. Paul realized that the enemy could and would take advantage of even the slightest glitch in his armor in just the same way that David had taken advantage of the almost unnoticeable breach in the giant's protection. Therefore, he constantly made sure that he kept his tamperproof seal intact through carefully guarding his conscience.   If we violate His conviction, we break the protective seal on our lives. Once that seal is broken, we cannot enter spiritual battle with the full confidence as before. We might say that we can't live like hell and expect heaven's results. If the seal is broken, we must have it reapplied in accordance to the promise of I John 1:9 that we have already noted, "If we confess our sins, he is faithful and just to forgive us our sins, and to cleanse us from all unrighteousness."

Supernatural Wisdom and Revelation

In Ephesians 1:17, Paul prayed that we would have wisdom and revelation in the knowledge of our Lord Jesus Christ. He realized that, unlike simple factual knowledge, these truths were more realistically "caught" than taught. Until we have that spirit of wisdom, revelation, and knowledge, we are not in a place to do proper spiritual warfare. If we don't know by divine revelation that we have these precious promises Paul has been teaching us about, they will not benefit us in our spiritual conflict.

Once, I took my wife to a nice restaurant for a delicious dinner. As I was getting into the car to leave the parking lot, I suddenly remembered a coupon in my pocket for a free meal at that restaurant. My buy-one-get-one-free coupon did me absolutely no good, even though I had it with me. I paid full price because I didn't exercise the benefits of the coupon. Until we have the wisdom, revelation, and knowledge so that we know who we are and what is our position in Christ, we aren't prepared to fight. We will try to pay the bill when Jesus has already paid it in full for us. We will be doing things in our own flesh and soulical power and we will probably be defeated by the devil in the process. The power of our position is tied to the fact that we have a spirit of wisdom, a spirit of understanding, and a spirit of knowledge that tells us who we are.

A British pastor who ran a home for the elderly members of his church was on one of his routine visits to the home when he stopped to chat with an illiterate woman who had been taken off the streets and placed in this home as a charity case. As he was visiting with her, he noticed something pinned to the wall and asked her what it was. She said that it was a picture of the queen of England, which a wealthy gentleman whom she had once served as a cook and housekeeper had given to her. Before he died, the man had given her a beautiful picture of the queen. Because she couldn't read, she didn't know that it wasn't just a picture of the queen of England; it was a bank note worth a lot of money! She was actually a very wealthy woman with enough money to take care of all of her own expenses, but did not have wisdom, revelation, and knowledge to know that she was living far below her capabilities.

Paul told us that he wass praying for us to have this spirit of wisdom, revelation, and knowledge working in us in the knowledge of Him "that ye may know what is the hope of his calling, and what the riches of the glory of his inheritance in the saints." If we do not have a spirit of wisdom, revelation, and knowledge, we do not have this understanding and cannot know the hope of our calling and how we should be living. Remember that in verse eight, he told us that it was through wisdom and prudence that we would be able to experience the lavish blessings of God.

One of the things that we must come to realize is that "the working of His mighty power" is within us.

> And what is the exceeding greatness of his power to us-ward who believe, according to the working of his mighty power. (verse 1:19)

Notice that verse twenty says that this exceeding great power has already been wrought, or put into play. It came into effect when Christ was raised from the dead. This is the essence of the gospel! The word "gospel" means "good news"; it is the reporting of good things that have already happened. When we turn on the television or pick up the newspaper, we see what has already happened -- not what is going to happen. In the same way, we need to search the scriptures to see what has already happened -- not what might happen in the future. Unfortunately, far too many of us read the promises of God from the viewpoint that He might someday in the sweet by-and-by bless us with healing, deliverance, prosperity, etc. In reality, all these things have already been provided; they are part of the gospel -- the news that has already happened. We just need to change our vantage point. Instead of seeing ourselves down on the same level with our problems, we need to begin to see ourselves as already raised with Christ and seated with Him in the heavenly places far above all the works of the enemy. We need to see ourselves as participants in a victory that has already been won. There is exceeding power, and it works through us according to God's very own mighty power. When we go into a spiritual confrontation, if we think that we are going in on our own power, we don't have any hope of being victorious. The truth of the matter is that whatever works in us is according to God's power. We have the spirit of wisdom, revelation, and knowledge so that we can have the comprehension that the power working in us is God's power. Paul calls it "exceeding" power. It is not just barely enough power. It is more than enough power. If we had begun our study on spiritual warfare at chapter six verse ten, our focus would have been on the power of our enemy as is mentioned in verse twelve. However, since we started at the beginning rather than at the end, our focus is now on the exceeding great power we have in comparison to the enemy's simple power.

Paul prayed for us continually that we would have this spirit of revelation, wisdom, and understanding so that we can begin to appreciate and live in this exceeding power of God "which he wrought in Christ, when he raised him from the dead, and set him at his own right hand in the heavenly places." (verse 1:20)

The climax of this section of Paul's discussion focuses on the fact that Jesus is far above all principalities.

> Far above all principality, and power, and might, and dominion, and every name that is named, not only in this world, but also in that which is to come. (verse 1:21)

We are blessed with all spiritual blessings in heavenly places because we are seated with Jesus in the heavenly places. Since He is seated far above every principality, power, might, and dominion, and every name that is named

-- so are we!

We must understand the forces that we, as Christians, have to deal with: they are principalities; they are spiritual forces -- kings with armies of warriors. When some Christians learn about this enemy, they have a wrong concept of warfare and respond in fear because they haven't built a solid spiritual foundation for encountering the enemy. This foundation starts back in Ephesians chapter one where Paul says that Christ is far above these principalities. He is not just a little bit above them; rather, He is far above them. I understand that a marble dropped from the top of the Empire State Building would break through the concrete sidewalk below. That's the power of being positioned far above rather than just being elevated by a few inches or feet.

We are not coming into the battle on equal ground. It is not "maybe so, maybe no." On the contrary, we know that those principalities and powers are already under our feet. We don't have to be intimidated by their names or their positions, and we don't have to be in fear of their faces! II Corinthians 2:14 declares that Christ always -- not sometimes -- causes us to triumph. We miss this pertinent and powerful truth if we begin our study on spiritual warfare at the "finally." By starting our study with Ephesians 6:10, we are focused on the principalities mentioned in verse twelve rather than the fact that we are already positioned in a far superior position of authority than these principalities could ever achieve.

If we don't have the revelation of how strong we are and how beloved we are to God and that He has seated us above the enemy principalities, we will involve ourselves in an unnecessary fight and return home beaten and bruised on a stretcher, or even in a spiritual body bag. On the other hand, if we have this revelation we will go into that warfare with a different kind of a mentality -- the "I'm more than a conqueror" attitude.

Our Transformation from the Kingdom of Darkness

The next foundational area that must be clarified is that we understand our transformation. We were not always in this position of authority and power. We have been transformed by being brought from another position and placed into this position. If we don't understand that we have been transformed -- changed from who we were -- we cannot adequately enter into spiritual warfare.

If we go back through the Old Testament, we will find example after example of Israel's finding themselves under bondage to their enemies (the Egyptians, Philistines, Assyrians, Babylonians, etc.). Before Israel experienced deliverance, they had to repent so that God could deliver them. When Ezra saw that Israel had intermarried with the Canaanites, he fell on his knees until the time of the evening sacrifice. (Ezra 9:4) He recognized the wickedness of the people and interceded for the people to be restored. Nehemiah did the same thing. (Nehemiah 1:4) Daniel also prayed and interceded for his people. (Daniel 9:3)

We must have the revelation that we also used to be in bondage, but now God has set us free from that bondage so that we can rightly assume our position of authority. Popular Christian "buzz" words have been, "I'm just a sinner saved by grace," or "Everybody has to sin a little bit every day; after all, we are still human." Neither of these statements is true. When a parishioner made reference to being a "sinner saved by grace," the pastor reached out his hand and said, "This is my dirty hand washed with soap." It didn't take an involved theology lesson to get the point across; he simply helped the gentleman see the obvious: if we are in Christ, we are no longer old sinners we once were; instead we are totally new creatures! We have been brought out of the kingdom of darkness and translated into the kingdom of His dear Son. We have to realize that we are no longer sinners but are now saints. There used to be some sinners who had bodies that looked a lot like ours, but those old men are dead and buried in the waters of baptism, and we have been raised as a new creatures who are totally free. We have no excuse to sin because we have been made into totally different creatures by the working of God's grace.

We have to realize our transformation -- where we have been brought from and that we have indeed been brought out. Awesome power is added to our lives and ministries when we realize that transformation. The ex-prostitute, the ex-drug addict, and the ex-sinner have powerful ministries to those still held in the bondage of prostitution, drug abuse, and sin. To this end, Paul made twelve points for us to consider.

> And you hath he quickened, who were dead in trespasses and sins; Wherein in time past ye walked according to the course of this world, according to the prince of the power of the air, the spirit that now worketh in the children of disobedience. (verse 2:1-2)

The only enemy we don't have to be concerned about is a dead one. Remember all the scenes in the war movies where the soldiers simply walk across the dead bodies of the enemies who were fighting against them so violently just minutes before. There was a time when we were like those dead soldiers in the movie; we were spiritually dead because of our sins. At that time, the devil did not have to fear us as an enemy; he could walk all over us just like the scene in the movie. But now -- in a reversal of the war movie episode -- we are alive in Christ, and he shakes in his boots when he sees us begin to flex our spiritual muscles. That's a transformation! At one time we walked according to the way the devil wanted us to walk. We need to realize that we were (past tense) subject to these forces, but we no longer are (present tense).

When we make a change, we cannot continue to live

the way we lived before the change. We used to be dead; now we are alive. We used to walk according to the prince of the power of the air. Although he still rules in the sons of disobedience, he does not rule in us. We no longer live in his kingdom; we live in another kingdom. When I lived in Indiana, I paid my tax payments to the State of Indiana. Now that I live in Colorado, I no longer send my taxes to Indiana. In the same way, we must learn that we no longer owe any dues to the devil!

The second reality concerning our transformation is that we at one time fulfilled the lusts of the flesh and of the mind.

> Among whom also we all had our conversation in times past in the lusts of our flesh, fulfilling the desires of the flesh and of the mind; and were by nature the children of wrath, even as others. (verse 2:3)

At one time we used to fulfill the lusts of the fleshly and soulical parts of our personalities, but we don't have to do that any more. Paul tells us that to be spiritually minded is life and peace, but to be carnally minded is death. (Romans 8:6) We are now walking in the spirit -- and, if so, we will not fulfill carnal lusts. (Galatians 5:16) We now live by the spirit man who walks in the direction of the Holy Spirit. I have a little illustration that I enjoy presenting occasionally to help people understand what it means to live and walk in the spirit. Holding a piano tuning fork in each hand, I strike one of them against the edge of the table and bring it close to the one in my other hand. Almost like magic, the second tuning fork will suddenly start "singing the same song" as the first one. Because they are both tuned to the same pitched musical note, the vibrations from the first one sets up resonance in the second one -- and it begins to give off the same note as the first one. When we have been changed into the image of Christ through the Lord's regenerative work, we begin to resonate at the same vibration with the Holy Spirit. We are no longer subject to the patterns of the world; instead, we march to the beat of the Holy Spirit's drum!

Point three is that we have been made alive together with Christ.

> Even when we were dead in sins, hath
> quickened us together with Christ, (by
> grace ye are saved.) (verse 2:5)

The King James Version says that we are "quickened" from the deadness of sins. We are made alive. We have been resurrected. That is a transformation! We were dead in sins, but now we are resurrected to life.

The fourth truth is that we sit in heavenly places in Christ Jesus.

> And hath raised us up together, and made
> us sit together in heavenly places in Christ
> Jesus. (verse 2:6)

Prior to Jesus' death and resurrection, He was subject to human limitations. Although His life and ministry were characterized by the miraculous, it was only after His sojourn in the grave that He proclaimed, "All power is given unto me in heaven and in earth." (Matthew 28:18) Paul said that we have been raised with Christ and that we share in the post-resurrection authority. When Jesus sat down in the heavenly places, He began to exercise His authoritative position; we are offered to share in that exercise with Him.

Paul next introduces the concept that we are the workmanship of God.

> For we are his workmanship, created in
> Christ Jesus unto good works, which God
> hath before ordained that we should walk in
> them. (verse 2:10)

We are no longer the old man who was the workmanship of the devil. When the devil wanted to turn us this way or that, he had the right to mold us as he wished because we were his subjects. Now we are under Christ's working. Now He has the right to mold us as He wishes. If He wants to put the glory of God upon us, He has the right to do it. If He wants to put the righteousness of God into us,

He can do it. He is the one who is molding us. He is the potter, and we are the clay. The great part of that truth is that He has a good plan already pre-designed for our lives. (Jeremiah 29:11) We used to walk according to the will of the devil, now we are being reworked by God and we can begin to walk according to the new nature.

Point six is simply that we are drawn very close to God through His blood.

> But now in Christ Jesus ye who sometimes
> were far off are made nigh by the blood of
> Christ. (verse 2:13)

When you were a child, were you ever attacked by a bully or chased by a dog? Horrifying wasn't it? But, remember how good it felt and how secure you were when you able to get close to your dad? Being near him instantly mitigated the threat of the bully and the dog! The same is true in our spiritual lives; when we draw near to God, we have the confidence it takes to be able to resist the devil. At one time we were aliens from the covenants, without hope and without God, but now we are in Christ. We were at one time afar off, but we have now been brought nigh. At one time, we were outside the promises of God. We didn't have the covenant, we didn't have a relationship with God, and we were afar off. Now we are brought close to God through the blood of Jesus Christ.

The seventh point follows closely on the previous one: we have been made fellow citizens with the saints.

> Now therefore ye are no more strangers
> and foreigners, but fellowcitizens with the
> saints, and of the household of God. (verse
> 2:19)

Our transformation is that at one time we were strangers and foreigners to God, but now we have a new citizenship. According to I Corinthians 15:50, we are no longer citizens of the kingdom of flesh and blood -- which explains why we no longer wrestle against flesh and blood. We have been naturalized into the kingdom of the Son of

God (Colossians 1:13) and have our citizenship in heaven (Philippians 3:20) that is characterized by righteousness, peace, and joy (Romans 14:17).

In my work as a college dean, I've had plenty of opportunity to see first-hand the power of citizenship. When the students from foreign countries would come here to study, their visas restricted them from working in the country. When the international students would come to my office to ask for assistance in finding employment, I would have to flatly refuse them -- unlike the American students whom I could readily help locate more work than they could handle. It wasn't a matter of discrimination; it was a matter of citizenship.

In biblical times, Roman citizenship meant that no matter where you were, you lived with all the rights and privileges as if you were in Rome itself. When Paul was about to be beaten, he asked if it were lawful for them to do such a thing since he was a Roman citizen. (Acts 22:25) The persecutor backed off because one of Paul's privileges as a Roman citizen was that he could not be beaten or whipped without a fair trial. Before the apostle announced his citizenship, the soldier sneered as he readied the thongs to lash across his victim's back. As soon as he heard that Paul was a Roman citizen, he cowered and stuttered as he apologized. When the Jewish authorities were going to lynch him, he demanded that Caesar hear his case. (verse 25:11) All the power, all the resources, and all the forces of the Roman Empire began to work in Paul's advantage to take him all the way from Israel to Rome for the very emperor himself to hear his case -- all because he had citizenship. If Paul had not had citizenship, he could have been destroyed.

We must walk into spiritual warfare with the revelation that we have citizenship in heaven. We may be in America or in Europe or in Asia; but spiritually, we are seated in heaven and have fellow citizenship with the saints. Our transformation to heaven's citizenship roll can become the guarantee that we, like Paul, have an entire empire at our beckon call! As citizens, we must learn to appeal to our privileges listed in our "Bill of Rights" including such provisions as Deuteronomy 28:7 (The LORD shall cause thine enemies that rise up against thee to be smitten before thy face: they shall come out against thee one way, and flee before thee seven ways.), Psalm 91:7-8 (A thousand shall fall at thy side, and ten thousand at thy right hand; but it shall not come nigh thee. Only with thine eyes shalt thou behold and see the reward of the wicked.), and Isaiah 54:17 (No weapon that is formed against thee shall prosper; and every tongue that shall rise against thee in judgment thou shalt condemn. This is the heritage of the servants of the LORD, and their righteousness is of me, saith the LORD.)

The fact that we are now the habitation of God is Paul's eighth point.

> In whom ye also are builded together for an
> habitation of God through the Spirit. (verse
> 2:22)

At one time we were strangers, but now we are God's very dwelling place. God Himself lives inside of us. It really seems difficult to imagine the possibility of defeat or failure when you realize that God Himself is inside us.

Grasping hold of that point results in the next point that Paul gave in verse twelve.

> In whom we have boldness and access
> with confidence by the faith of him.

We have boldness and access because we are members of the family and because we have citizenship rights. There should be no hesitation for us to approach God because we can enter into His presence with confidence by faith, but how much more is the boldness when we realize that the God we wish to approach has made His dwelling right inside of us!

Point number ten re-emphasized the indwelling of Christ in us, when Paul said that Christ dwells in our hearts by faith.

> That Christ may dwell in your hearts by
> faith; that ye, being rooted and grounded in
> love. (verse 3:17)

His eleventh point speaks of the stability we must develop in this transformation reality -- we are rooted and grounded in faith.

In Ephesians 3:17-19, Paul told us that we now have Christ dwelling in our hearts by faith and we are rooted and grounded in the faith and that we know the unknowable love of God. These things are the result of our transformation. Before we were transformed, Christ was not living in us. We were not rooted and grounded in our faith, and we did not know the love of God. But because of this transformation, we have become totally new creatures that are alive to tremendous reality. We can now go into spiritual warfare with confidence and strength so that we have no question as to who will win.

The final point in this section brings us to a reality that cannot even be comprehended -- much less experienced -- short of being transformed: we know the unknowable love of Christ.

> And to know the love of Christ, which
> passeth knowledge, that ye might be filled
> with all the fulness of God. (verse 3:19)

In this section on our transformation, Paul started out by saying that at one time we used to be subject to the enemy whom we are now going to fight. Thus, we can walk into spiritual warfare with a different relationship to the enemy. If we really know all these truths before we get to the "finally" of verse ten of chapter six, we will walk into the battle knowing that we are now no longer under the authority of our opponent even though we were once subject to his power.

Our Position in the Body of Christ

Early on in his letter, Paul has already introduced the next truth that he will now expound. Here he begins to apply the principle to the warfare we are to enter.

> Wherefore I also, after I heard of your faith in the Lord Jesus, and love unto all the saints. (verse 1:15)

It is important for us to function within the Body of Christ to be able to do spiritual warfare. Very few times do we read of successful soldiers who went out on "Lone Ranger" expeditions; yet, history is full of the success stories of soldiers who functioned within the entire army. We cannot just go out and do spiritual warfare on our own. Instead, we are commissioned to link together for security, support, and success. In biblical times when the soldiers went out to war, they had shields with an interlinking hook-and-eye system. By interlocking their shields, the soldiers formed one great mobile wall. They became a human tank marching forward toward their enemy with their shields as one solid wall of protection. If one man stood alone and held his shield in front of himself, he was still in grave danger from his enemy because the blows could come at him from every direction. Unless he was very agile and quick, he could be struck from the left when he was using his shield to guard himself from a blow from the right. However, when he was joined by soldiers on his right and left, his companions and their shields guarded him on the right and left -- making him invulnerable. The fascinating realization is that neither of his companions needed to be great muscle men; all that was needed was for them to be in their places, securely fastened to him. Just the fact that they were there covered his vulnerable spots. One contemporary Christian song expresses the necessity of this same principle in the Body of Christ, "I need you to survive."

Since the armament described in Ephesians chapter six is all frontal gear, it is absolutely necessary that we have brothers and sisters linked to us on our right and left; otherwise, we are in danger of the enemy's blows. As we link together in a group effort, synergism (the whole is greater than the sum of the parts) occurs. This is why we are told that two can chase ten thousand while one can chase only a thousand. (Deuteronomy 32:30) Remember, God is in the business of building army, not just collecting soldiers.

When Paul spoke of the shield of faith, he said that it was above everything else. Some versions emphasize that the shield is above all because it is in front of the other elements; other translations imply that the shield is the most important part of the armament and, therefore "above all else." Regardless of the interpretation, once we realize that it is the shield that links us to the rest of the Body of Christ in order to bring us to mutual strength and protection, we can see why Paul says that it is above all else. As individual warriors, we would each have to struggle against our opponent; however, as a united force, we are able to solidly stand our ground. Notice that Paul addresses "my brethren" when he admonishes us to take up the armor of God. He does not speak to us as individuals but as a corporate body with this plural noun. Putting on the armor of God is a corporate function of the entire body of faith.

We must learn to live and work together within the Body of Christ without concern for the carnal differences that tend to divide us. If you saw the movie, Wind Talkers, you will remember how difficult it was for the soldiers to overcome their prejudices and accept the Navajo recruits. Many of the white soldiers had grandfathers who had fought in the battles against the American Indians and they had all grown up playing "cowboys and Indians"; therefore, it was hard for them to see the Navajo soldiers as their comrades rather than their enemies. But you'll also remember that it was these very Native American radio operators who saved the lives of the men who were so resistant to having them as comrades. These Native American recruits played a significant role in winning the war because the Axis intelligence forces weren't able to decode the messages when they were transmitted in the Navajo language. What's true in the natural army is especially true in the spiritual army: we must establish unity within the Body of Christ because our lives depend upon what the other members (very often the ones whom we don't want to befriend in our natural selves) can supply.

Paul says that we are to walk worthy of our calling. (verse 4:1) We must not walk outside of what God has called us to do. We should not walk in disrespect for what God has called us to. Instead we are to walk in a lifestyle that matches up to our calling. Each soldier must recognize his position and fulfill it with the greatest dignity, diligence, and deftness.

Next, the apostle began to give us some pointers on how we can walk in a way that will make others willing to link together with us. Lowliness, humility, and the practice of edifying one another in love are qualities that make others willing to cement themselves to us.

> With all lowliness and meekness, with longsuffering, forbearing one another in love. (verse 4:2)

The devil knows the power of pride. It was pride that destroyed him (Isaiah 14:13-15), and pride has become one of his most powerful tools he uses to destroy others (Proverbs 16:18). Nebuchadnezzar, whom God Himself called the head of gold among the empires of history, became like a wild beast because he allowed pride to control him. (Daniel 4:28-33)

Here, Paul amplified our calling and responsibility as members of the Body of Christ. He told us that walking worthily has to do with our relationship to those people around us. It is not only a matter of restraining from sin that makes us worthy of our calling. It also has to do with being lowly, gentle, patient, and forbearing. It has to do with upholding one another and blending in with the Body of

Christ. We are called to link arms with our brothers as part of this unified force.

Humility draws people together while pride drives wedges between them. We can't have unity without humility, and we can't stand without unity -- meaning that humility is foundational for the church to survive and thrive. Dr. Lester Sumrall used a clever little saying to emphasize the significance of staying in our places in the Body of Christ, "The first banana to leave the bunch is the one that's going to get skinned." We must get to the point that we realize that we need each other in order to survive. No one is an island, standing alone. Instead, we must realize that we are more like men in a boat. Perhaps that is why we refer to ourselves as being in fellowship -- several fellows all in the same ship!

Once we have this paradigm shift, we'll understand the significance of this little Jewish fable. It seems that a man took out a drill while the boat was in the middle of the sea and began boring a hole in the hull underneath his seat. When the other passengers began to panic and ask what he thought he was doing, he replied, "But the hole is only under my own seat." Unfortunately, too many of us fail to see that nothing we do affects only us and that nothing that anyone else does occurs without affecting the rest of us. The power of each individual Christian is actually the power of the whole Body of Christ working together. Out of the American Revolution was birthed the phrase, "United we stand; divided we fall." A modern reworking of that expression proclaims, "Divided we stand; united we fall," emphasizing the fact that we are all destined to collapse if we try to stand individually rather than as a unified whole. Paul was insistent that we understand the vital importance of being a unified body when he told us in verses four through six that

> There is one body, and one Spirit, even as
> ye are called in one hope of your calling;
> One Lord, one faith, one baptism, One God

and Father of all, who is above all, and
through all, and in you all.

Unfortunately, the Body of Christ continues to allow simple things like baptism to divide us. Many Christians totally lob off whole segments of the Body simply because they baptize in the names of all the members of the Trinity while others baptize only in the name of Jesus. Dr. Sumrall once ministered for a congregation for a full week but was asked to leave the building when the church took communion on Sunday simply because he had not been baptized the same way they were.

Ephesians 4:2 talks about making sure inside ourselves that we are the kind of people who can link arms with one another. He says that we are to have the right attitude and not to get heady and high-minded, which would prevent us from linking together with the other brethren. In verse three, Paul tells us to put forth the effort to see that this unity is maintained. We are to do what it takes to make our brothers able to link together with us. He tells us to do everything we can to keep unity in the Spirit so that other Christians will be willing to link with us. The term "endeavoring" means working hard. Keeping a bond of peace and unity in the Spirit with our brothers is not an easy job; we must work hard at it.

Paul stated in his next point that there are certain God-appointed leadership positions in the Body of Christ.

And he gave some, apostles; and some,
prophets; and some, evangelists; and
some, pastors and teachers. (verse 4:11)

There are different functions within the Body. As we have seen, it is important for everybody to link together, but there still has to be someone who calls the shots and gives the directives. Just like in a natural army, we need people in leadership positions so that we can function as the Body. When Paul talked about these leadership positions -- the fivefold ministry gifts -- he told us why God put these leaders into the church: "For the perfecting of the saints, for the work of the ministry, for the edifying of the body of Christ: Till we all come in the unity of the faith, and of the knowledge of the Son of God, unto a perfect man, unto the measure of the stature of the fulness of Christ." (verses 12-13) Their purpose in the Body is not so that they can be exalted, but so that they can perfect the saints to the point that we are no longer tossed to and fro by every wind of doctrine but rather are made into the stature and fullness of Christ. (verses 14-15)

The purpose of the drill sergeant is not so he can look important but to bring the individual soldiers into one army moving with total unity of purpose. Going into spiritual warfare without properly submitting to spiritual leadership could become a suicide mission. The purpose of the fivefold ministry is to bring the Body into unity. As we have already seen, being one united force is the key to strength and victory. First John 5:4 declares that the victory we have to overcome the world is our faith. With these realities in mind, we can see how vitally important it is that we have godly leadership to bring us to that unity in the faith -- an interlocking shield of faith that protects the entire church as well as each individual member.

Paul next turned to the words we speak.

But speaking the truth in love, may grow up
into him in all things, which is the head,
even Christ. (verse 4:15)

Words can heal or kill. How often a little word of encouragement has saved a ministry, a marriage, a man. Unfortunately, it is probably more often that the lack of such a word has allowed discouragement to destroy many more ministries, marriages, and men. Although constructive criticism is the foundation for correction, negative and criticizing words carry lethal poisons. Edifying words are words of truth that are spoken in love with the benefit of the Body of Christ as the motivation.

At this last point in this section, we come back to our illustration of the Roman soldiers with their moving wall of shields. Here Paul said that we, as the Body of Christ, are "fitly joined together."

> From whom the whole body fitly joined together and compacted by that which every joint supplieth, according to the effectual working in the measure of every part, maketh increase of the body unto the edifying of itself in love. (verse 4:16)

We are expected to come to the place where there is one whole body -- not a soldier here and a soldier there -- but all the soldiers coming together as one compact unit with every joint (every member) doing what it is supposed to do.

The picture of the Roman soldiers marching together shows each one as a joint, a flexible place where each shield hooks into the eye of the neighbor's shield. However when all of them were hooked together there was a connectedness that allowed them to move forward as one solid army. Perhaps the reason Paul described us as joints rather than bones was because so much "hinges" on us and we must be careful not to get "out of joint" with one another.

In Ezekiel chapter thirty-seven, God showed the prophet a vision of a valley filled with dry bones. They were lifeless and useless until the prophet prophesied to them and the Spirit moved upon them. At that instant they came together -- as the old song says, with the toe bone connected to the foot bone, the foot bone connected to the anklebone…all the way to the head bone! Once they came together, verse ten said that the reconstructed soldiers stood up on their feet. That is exactly what Paul is trying to birth inside us as members of the Body of Christ: if we will only come together in the unity of the Spirit we will be able to stand as God's great army. It is interesting that the thing that brought these dried up bones together and then brought them to life was the words of the prophet. Paul emphasized here that it is the words of truth that we speak through love that will bring the same result in the Body of

Christ. Notice how Ezekiel summarizes the results of restoration of these bones -- "an exceeding great army." (verse 10) That's exactly the results we can expect when we apply the principles the Apostle Paul is giving us here.

An old saying goes, "The chain is only as strong as its weakest link." Each person in the Body of Christ has to realize, "I am very important to the whole because if I am weak that is exactly where we are going to fall apart." If there is any place where somebody is not hinged into the next one, we are leaving an empty hole for the devil's forces to come in. Just as a thief breaks in through a window or door rather than blasting through the solid wall, the devil will always attack at the weakest point. We must recognize the importance of keeping a strong link with every member. If you aren't there, I'm not protected; if I am not there, you are not protected. For your benefit as well as my own benefit, I have to do everything I can to link together with you in the bond of peace. I have to do everything I know to keep love and unity between us. If I don't have you, I am wide open for attack; if you don't have me, you are also vulnerable. We must endeavor to keep the bond of peace.

The reason God saw fit to give apostles, prophets, evangelists, pastors, and teachers to the Body of Christ is so that we can grow up until we learn how to fit together in this full-grown Body. Twice, the apostle uses the word "perfect" in reference to the job that the fivefold ministry is to accomplish. Verse twelve says that they are to perfect the saints, and verse thirteen says that they are to bring the Body of Christ into a perfect man. When we realize that the Greek word for "perfect" means mature, we are able to see a very significant point about what it is that makes the Body of Christ work -- maturity. Mature people are able to get over their differences. Mature people are able to work together with people from different backgrounds or with different opinions about things. Mature people are able to see the bigger picture of what is best for the whole community rather than to look for what will benefit them individually.

There was a centurion who came to Jesus for the healing of his sick servant. (Matthew 8:1) This military officer knew that Jesus didn't have to physically come to his house. He understood that Jesus had the authority to stand in any place and wage spiritual warfare miles away by simply speaking the Word. The centurion was convinced that his servant would be healed even without Jesus' presence in his room. He explained to Jesus, "I am a man who is under authority." He was saying that he understood the spiritual principles because of his position under a commander above him who gives an order that the centurion immediately obeys. It is likely that this Roman officer really disliked the idea of having to leave the fertile valleys of Italy to serve in the deserts of Palestine. However, he submitted without complaint when handed the deployment orders. Having a proper relationship with his superiors, he could expect those under him to obey his commands because they also had a proper relationship with his authority. Because he worked within a "body" of soldiers, he understood spiritual authority. He knew that Jesus did not have to come to his house and physically shake the demon off of his servant or slap the sickness out of the man. He understood that Jesus had the authority so that when He commanded the spirit or illness to go He could expect it to obey. This revelation is very important. Our spiritual warfare is not in slapping and shaking. Jesus did not have to become physically involved with the servant, yet He could do spiritual warfare. Our spiritual warfare is using the same spiritual authority as Jesus because we are members of His Body. The authority of the Head flows through the whole Body as long as there are no breaks and divisions to hinder its flow. We might think of it as electricity flowing through a wire; as long as there are no disconnected points, the voltage is just as strong at any point along the circuit as it is at the generator. In the properly connected Body of Christ, each member can minister with the full authority of Jesus Himself. That is why we are taught to pray in the name of Jesus -- exerting His full authority into every prayer we pray.

Much of the teaching today relates to physical involvement in spiritual warfare, but that is not what Paul taught. If we understand our relationship to God, our transformation from the kingdom of darkness, and our position within the Body, we are prepared to do spiritual warfare with tremendous authority.

Realizing the New Creation Within Us

We have to realize that we are new creatures in Christ. We are not just a more recent version of the old creature, but we are an entirely different creation from what we were before. We cannot keep the bond of peace and come into unity in the Body as long as we are old creatures trying to be patched up. We will only keep the bond of peace when we become new creatures, realize what our new creation is all about, and get rid of the old things that were part of the old man -- the anger, hostility, and pride. When we move out the old creation and move in the new creation that is made new in the love of Christ, then we are able to keep the bond of peace.

Paul made seven observations about the new creation in rather rapid-fire succession.

First, we no longer walk in the vanity of our minds.

> This I say therefore, and testify in the Lord, that ye henceforth walk not as other Gentiles walk, in the vanity of their mind. (verse 4:17)

Second, we are no longer ignorant.

> Having the understanding darkened, being alienated from the life of God through the ignorance that is in them, because of the blindness of their heart. (verse 4:18)

Third, we are no longer lascivious, unclean, or greedy.

> Who being past feeling have given themselves over unto lasciviousness, to work all uncleanness with greediness. (verse 4:19)

Fourth, we are taught the truth in and through Jesus.

> But ye have not so learned Christ; If so be that ye have heard him, and have been taught by him, as the truth is in Jesus. (verse 4:20-21)

Fifth, we must put off the old sinful actions, habits, and thought patterns.

That ye put off concerning the former conversation the old man, which is corrupt according to the deceitful lusts. (verse 4:22)

Sixth, the makeover comes in the area of having our minds under the control of our spirit man.

And be renewed in the spirit of your mind. (verse 4:23)

Seventh, we have to take deliberate action in putting the new creation personality, character, and qualities into effect in our lives.

And that ye put on the new man, which after God is created in righteousness and true holiness. (verse 4:24)

When believers were baptized in the first century church, they did not just go into the water and come back up out of the water. There was another step they followed that we don't use today. The new believers would wear their old dirty coats to the baptismal waters. Many times, their coats were stained and tattered. When they would go into the water, they would take their old coats off and throw them back to the shore. When they came up out of the water, there would be somebody standing there ready to put new coats on them. These new garments would be perfectly white, sparkling clean robes. Baptism symbolized the burial and resurrection, but it also demonstrated the taking off of the old man and the putting on of the new man. They came to the river looking like normal people, but they walked out of the water looking like saints.

When Paul used the illustration of taking off the old and putting on the new, every believer who had ever seen a baptism understood perfectly what he was saying. There was a process to putting on the new coat during baptism. The new coat didn't automatically just come upon them; there was a conscious effort to place one arm in a sleeve, then to put the other arm into the other sleeve, and then to pull the coat into proper place. The same thing is the case with our new nature in Christ. When we get born again, we do become new creatures automatically. However, there must also be an effort on our part to pull off the old ways and let them drop away. We have to be conscious to the fact that there are things we don't want in our lives -- attitudes, characteristics, and personality traits. At the same time, we have to consciously put on the new garment. Where does this process take place? Paul tells us that this change comes through the renewing in the spirit of our mind. (verse 4:23) At first reading this passage seems to say that there is a spirit of the mind -- something separate from our human spirit. In actuality, a more accurate way of translating this passage would emphasize "in the spirit" or "through the spirit." We must renew our minds through the spirit.

In another of his letters Paul wrote, "But as it is written, Eye hath not seen, nor ear heard, neither have entered into the heart of man, the things which God hath prepared for them that love him. But God hath revealed them unto us by his Spirit: for the Spirit searcheth all things, yea, the deep things of God." (I Corinthians 2:9-10) It is the Spirit of God (who understands God, His characteristics, and what He is doing) who comes to us and reveals to us what is the mind of God and what are the hidden things that God has in store for us. It is through our spirit man, in tune with the Holy Spirit, that our minds are renewed. Our minds will not be renewed by listening to positive motivational tapes. Such tapes may change our minds, but they cannot renew our minds. Paul is talking about the renewing of the mind that can only take place in the spirit realm.

Francis Frangipane, in his book The Three Battlegrounds, made this comment about the battleground of the mind:

> You will remember that the location where
> Jesus was crucified was called "Golgotha,"
> which meant "place of the skull." If we will
> be effective in spiritual warfare, the first field
> of conflict where we must learn warfare is

the battleground of the mind; i.e., the "place of the skull." For the territory of the uncrucified thought life is the beachhead of satanic assault in our lives. To defeat the devil, we must be crucified in the place of the skull. We must be renewed in the spirit of our minds.

Paul made a statement towards this light in another of his epistles.

For to be carnally minded is death; but to be spiritually minded is life and peace. (Romans 8:6)

Paul said that our spiritual life is all about taking off and putting on. It is a matter of our actually making a change. He didn't tell us to have Jesus take it off and let Jesus put it on. He said for us to take off and for us to put on. Just as our clothes do not jump onto our bodies each morning and then back into the closet each evening, our thoughts, actions, and attitudes will not automatically change themselves without an effort on our part. We have to take the responsibilities in disciplining ourselves. Perhaps it would be easy to have somebody pray for us, pour oil on us, and knock us to the floor so that we could get up as saints, but the Bible doesn't say that this is the way to become renewed. Instead, it tells us that we are to take off the old man and that we are to put on the new man.

Becoming a saint in Christ requires that we put in some discipline. Too many people in the church are actually failures because they are depending on somebody else's prayers and faith as their answer. As good as those things are, the Bible tells us that our key to becoming the saints Jesus wants us to be is that we put some effort into taking off and putting on as we deliberately renew our own minds through the revelation of the Holy Spirit.

Radically Different from Our Old Unregenerate Man

When speaking of sinners around us, we often use the expression, "Except for the grace of God, there go I." Yes, that is true; however, the emphasis of that sentence must be on the "grace of God" not on the "except." Once we accept the grace of God, the except for the grace of God becomes insignificant. He totally regenerates us and begins to remake us in His image!

In his next several points, Paul addressed the issues of how radically different the new man is from the old, unregenerate one. The first area is a renewed tongue.

> Wherefore putting away lying, speak every man truth with his neighbour: for we are members one of another. (verse 4:25)

The second area deals with a renewed emotion.

> Be ye angry, and sin not: let not the sun go down upon your wrath. (verse 4:26)

The next area of focus is renewed actions -- but more deeply, a renewed worldview.

> Let him that stole steal no more: but rather let him labour, working with his hands the thing which is good, that he may have to give to him that needeth. (verse 4:28)

If a man were a thief under the old law, the requirement would be that he pay back what he stole, but the new relationship says that he must get a legitimate job and work with his hands so that not only can he make restitution for his sin, but so that he can become a giver to those in need. If he is giving to needy people, he is doing something important in their lives -- he is stopping them from becoming thieves like he once was. The old creature who used to be a taker is now a giver. He is not a more recent version of the old man, but he is a radically different man.

Paul's next point here begins a second cycle of admonition where he again addresses a renewed tongue.

> Let no corrupt communication proceed out
> of your mouth, but that which is good to the
> use of edifying, that it may minister grace
> unto the hearers. (verse 4:29)

We used to be corrupt speakers. We could really give others a "piece of our mind" and tear people down by saying things that were against God and against His creation, but now out of our mouths comes edifying words of encouragement and uplifting. In order to build the Body of Christ, we must learn to speak out word that bless and encourage others. G. B. Stern once wrote, "Silent gratitude isn't much use to anyone." Robert Braut added, "There is no such thing as gratitude unexpressed. If it is unexpressed, it is plain, old-fashioned ingratitude." John F. Kennedy gave us a clear summation of the result of such expressions of edification, "As we express our gratitude, we must never forget that the highest appreciation is not to utter words, but to live by them."

At the next point, we are again brought to the issue of a renewed spiritual alignment. This time Paul addresses a totally different aspect.

> And grieve not the holy Spirit of God,
> whereby ye are sealed unto the day of
> redemption. Let all bitterness, and wrath,
> and anger, and clamour, and evil speaking,
> be put away from you, with all malice.
> (verse 4:30-31)

Next on this agenda is another admonition concerning the renewed emotion.

> And be ye kind one to another,
> tenderhearted, forgiving one another, even
> as God for Christ's sake hath forgiven you.
> (verse 4:32)

The following entry is again a discussion on renewed actions.

> Be ye therefore followers of God, as dear
> children. (verse 5:1)

Step by step we are following after God. We no longer follow the ways of the world (verse 4:17), but we are imitators and followers of God. We are still followers, but we are now following a new leader; we are now walking in God.

It is interesting that each of these transformations can play an important role in helping us to come into the unity within the Body that Paul has already stressed as being so necessary. We don't care to get too close to liars, but we love to be around people who are speaking edifying words. Angry people repel us, but peacemakers attract us. We always try to keep a distance from thieves, but we gravitate toward givers. If we think that they are going to reach into our pocket, we keep our distance, but we get close to those folks who have a habit of reaching into their own pockets.

In the middle of all this discussion about our own personal renewal, Paul brings it all back to spiritual conflict.

Neither give place to the devil. (verse 4:27)

We have to lock the door and tell him, "I resist you, and you are not coming into my life." At the same time we must be careful not to close the door of our lives on the Holy Spirit because our sensitivity to His voice is what ensures that we are preserved with that tamperproof seal.

And grieve not the holy Spirit of God, whereby ye are sealed unto the day of redemption. (verse 4:30)

--

Walking Circumspectly

In another context, Paul said for us to work out the salvation that is in us. (Philippians 2:12) There is a new creation that is inside of us, and we have to make an effort for it to come to the surface. We must work it out and make this new creation a reality and a demonstration in our lives.

In our position, we are not just to sit still and become "couch potatoes" in the kingdom of God. We are to take an offensive move and a forward aggression while we are in this position of authority. Paul began to discuss this very pointedly in Ephesians 5:14-5.

His first point concerning our offensive movement was that we must wake up and be aware.

> Wherefore he saith, Awake thou that sleepest, and arise from the dead, and Christ shall give thee light… (verse 5:14)

We are not to be settled "all snug in our beds" as the popular Christmas poem says. Instead, we are to awake from our sleep and let the light of Christ come through our lives.

His second point was that we walk circumspectly.

> See then that ye walk circumspectly, not as fools, but as wise. (verse 5:15)

Paul began to describe a forward advance, an offensive move. We are commanded to move forward. Sleepers are not moving forward. The dead are not moving forward. But we have awakened from our sleep and have risen from our deadness; we are starting to walk forward in our new spiritual position.

"Circumspectly" comes from the root word *circum*, meaning "around." It is from this word that we get such English words as "circumference" (the measurement around a circle) or "circumcision" (a cutting around). We get our word "spectacles" from the other root *spect*, which means "to see." To walk circumspectly is to walk looking around. We don't just walk aimlessly like a man sleepwalking.

A few years ago, several fighter pilots were doing

maneuvers in formation. One pilot lost his bearings and took a nosedive into the ground. Following the leader, all five of the other planes also crashed. What began as a routine training maneuver became a major tragedy. They did not walk circumspectly. On each one of those planes, there were instruments that told the pilots that they were headed for the ground, but the pilots ignored the instruments as they simply followed the leader.

Paul tells us that we are to be sure that we are walking circumspectly -- looking around and keeping our eyes open to see the traps, snares, and detours -- so that when we move, we do not move in the wrong direction. If we do not walk circumspectly, we walk as fools not knowing where we are going and what traps we are stepping into.

In thinking of the various kinds of traps I have seen used to capture wild animals, I noticed three interesting parallels with the ways the devil likes to capture his prey.

In Africa, there is a tribe of people who capture monkeys by placing a fistful of rice inside a coconut in which a very small hole has been drilled. The monkeys reach into the coconut to take the rice, but they soon find that they cannot pull their hands out of the coconut once their fists are closed around their treasured morsel of rice. Since the monkeys refuse to let go of their little treat, the hunters are able to easily capture them. I believe that the devil and his little helpers use this same kind of snare to bring millions of humans into captivity. If we would simply let go of the things we are holding on to, we could escape his snare. Sometimes, we hold on to habits that could easily be broken before they become addictions. Other times, we hold on to attitudes that could easily be changed unless they are allowed to remain until they become compulsions. Sometimes we hold on to physical things that must be released before they have us rather than our having them. No matter what the case, we are ensnared unless we learn to let go. We can free ourselves if we simply will!

Another snare that some hunters use is the pit trap in

which a roof of sticks and grass is laid over a deep hole in the ground. When the animal steps on the false floor, he falls through and is captured in the pit. I am reminded of a humorous story about two men who found themselves in just such a trap. It seems that one gentleman often cut through a cemetery as a shortcut from town to his home. One night, he fell into a new grave that had been dug since he last used his shortcut. After a number of unsuccessful attempts to get out, he reconciled himself to the idea that he would have to spend the night in the grave and wait for the morning when the workers would return. A while later, a second man had the same misfortune of taking the same shortcut and falling into the same open grave. Not noticing the first man in a dark corner of the grave, he set about to climb out of the hole. The first victim decided to watch a few minutes to see if the newcomer might find an escape route that he had missed. After a short while, he decided to warn the man that his attempts were futile, "Give up. There's no way out." But the second man instantly leapt all the way out of the pit and broke all previous track records racing out of the graveyard! It's the same way with many who are held in the devil's captivity -- all they need is for someone else to motivate them a little to break out of the imagined bondage which they think to be real. With a little "jump start," these people are often set free even without a prayer!

One final kind of snare is the mechanical trap that physically closes on its victim. A rabbit hutch, a bear trap, and a mousetrap would all be examples of this kind of snare. When captured in a trap of this sort, the victim cannot get free without outside help; someone else must open the door or release the spring and let him go free. This kind of deliverance can come only from a faith-filled believer who knows how to use the name of Jesus to cast out the demons that have taken control of the person's mind, body, or spirit. Fortunately, Jesus left us the authority to do just that. "And when he had called unto him his twelve disciples, he gave them power against unclean spirits, to cast them out, and to heal all manner of sickness and all manner of disease." (Matthew 10:1) "And these signs shall follow them that believe; In my name shall they cast out devils; they shall speak with new tongues." (Mark 16:17)

It is always important to remember that it really doesn't matter what kinds of traps the devil may set because the steps of a righteous man are ordered by the Lord (Psalm 37:23); He will walk us around them -- if we are led by the Spirit and walk circumspectly.

His third object of attention is mentioned in verse sixteen.

> Redeeming the time, because the days are evil.

We have to make all of our time count. We do not have the luxury of letting time be wasted. I find that little blocks of time are much more important than big blocks of time. Most people never complete the work they need to do because they are always waiting for those big blocks of three or four hours to start the project; it seems that such big blocks of time never come. Most people bypass bushels of small time segments and do nothing while waiting for that one big block of time. You may be waiting for twenty thousand dollars to buy a new car. The day may never come when someone hands you a twenty-thousand-dollar check. But you can get one hundred dollars at a time; put it in the bank; and then eventually you will have the money you need to buy the car. In the same way, you may never find a four-hour slot of time to do a project, but you can use the ten minutes here and ten minutes there.

The same is true in the kingdom of God. Many people just waste time. They don't witness to the person next to them on the bus or in the elevator because they are waiting for the time when they can stand up before a congregation of two or three hundred people to preach the gospel. The truth is that when we show ourselves faithful over the individual opportunities He places in our path, God will promote us to stand before the crowds.

Paul wanted us to understand that we live in an evil age and that we must, therefore, make every minute count for the Lord. We must look around and see what we need to be doing in this battle. Take every opportunity because these days are evil.

Knowing the Will of God

Next, Paul tells us that we must know the will of the Lord for our lives.

> Wherefore be ye not unwise, but understanding what the will of the Lord is.
> (verse 5:17)

We are unwise if we are unable to find the will of the Lord. We need to understand, prove, and move into the will of God in our daily lives. This is our offensive and aggressive stage in moving forward. How to recognize the will of the Lord is one of the most important things that any Christian can ever learn. We can come to know the will of the Lord in several ways.

The first and foremost way to know the will of the Lord is from the written Word. The written Word tells us what is the will of the Lord. For example, it is God's will that none shall perish but that all should come to everlasting life. (II Peter 3:9) If you are seated next to a sinner on the bus, what is the will of the Lord? The will of the Lord is that person next to you should not perish but for him to come to the knowledge of everlasting life. Therefore, the will of the Lord for you is that you should help that person move into the will of the Lord for his life. You don't have to ask God if it is His will for you to share the gospel with that person sitting next to you. You already have His will written in the Word, "Go ye into all the world, and preach the gospel to every creature." (Mark 16:15) The Word of God gives us general direction in what the will of the Lord is. We can study the Word and get a general revelation of God's will.

Don't get overly spiritual -- as some have done -- in seeking God's will. One man opened the Bible randomly and pointed his finger to a verse that read, "And Judas went out and hanged himself." (Matthew 27:5) He thought that he had better try again, so he closed his Bible, quickly opened it up again and randomly pointed his finger to another verse, "Go and do thou likewise." (Luke 10:37) Remembering that in the mouth of two or three witnesses everything is confirmed, again he closed his eyes, opened his Bible, and pointed his finger randomly to another verse. This time it read, "And what you do, do quickly." (John 13:27) This is certainly not the recommended method for understanding what God's Word would say concerning your life.

Another way the Lord reveals His will is through His Spirit. There is an inward witness inside each born-again believer to tell him what God wants for his individual life. God will speak to us, but it is very important for us to get to the place that we can hear the voice of the Lord. So many people come up to me saying, "If God would only show me what to do, I would do it." It is very likely that He is speaking, and they are not recognizing His voice. When we get very close and personal to the Lord, we are able to hear His voice.

Jesus said that His sheep would hear His voice and follow Him but would not follow a stranger. (John 10:3-5, 27) Notice that He said "sheep," not "lambs." We must mature in our relationship with the Lord in order to clearly recognize His voice. We must stay in close communion with Him so we will distinctly know His voice and obey it. Young lovers can talk for three or four hours about nothing at all. When their mothers ask what they have been doing and why they are coming in past their curfews, they reply, "Oh, we were just talking." It was not facts or knowledge that they were communicating; they were communicating relationship. The young man received something of the young lady's personality, and she received something of his personality through the time they spent together. Talking is very important in establishing a relationship -- with God as well as with other people. We need to get to the place that we can hear the voice of God and -- regardless of the circumstances under which that voice comes -- we know that it is the voice of God so that we are able to follow through with what He is saying. A mature Christian should be able to recognize the will of the Lord and not to be confused about it.

In Genesis chapter twenty-seven, we find the story of Isaac who had two sons, Esau and Jacob. We know that Isaac was old and blind, but the Bible doesn't say anything about his having hearing problems. He asked his son Esau to go hunting and bring back some venison for him. In the meantime, Jacob put on his brother's clothes in a plot to deceive the aged father. Isaac recognized that the voice was not the voice of Esau. Jacob smelled like Esau, he felt like Esau, but he didn't sound like Esau. Isaac denied that voice because it didn't match with the circumstances. He blessed the deceptive son because he didn't follow the voice that he heard. We should learn a valuable lesson from this Old Testament story -- obey the voice of God regardless of the circumstances!

Another way that we can know the will of God is through supernatural confirmation. God can use supernatural signs and wonders such as prophecy for confirmation of His will; however, He usually does not give us direction that way. Generally, He uses this form of communication as a confirmation of what He has already spoken to our hearts.

We can also know the will of God through the advice and counsel of elders. When there is something that you want to know or have a question about, bring it up before the eldership in your local church. We don't need to go to a leading televangelist for his opinion on it, we need to go to somebody who personally knows us and loves us enough to give us what is really in his heart. The evangelist may have a supernatural word that would associate to us, but our pastor or elder -- the person who has seen us mature and has spiritual oversight over us -- can go before God with a heart of care for us, and he will receive the answer from God.

One final way of knowing God's will is through the circumstances in which we find ourselves. For instance, Paul certainly didn't plan on getting himself bitten by a snake; but when it happened, he realized that God had set up the circumstances so that a revival could occur on the island. (Acts 28:3-10) Regardless of the method, it is imperative that we learn to know and follow the will of God for our lives and in our day-to-day affairs.

Offensive Movement

General Douglas McArthur said, "It is fatal to enter any war without the will to win." Our stance in this spiritual conflict is that we intend -- no, we expect -- to win. We are aggressively pursuing the gates of hell, knowing that they will not be able to withstand our offensive attack against them. (Matthew 16:18) We aggressively defy the enemy, knowing that he -- and never us -- will have to back down and even run away. (James 4:7)

Paul's fifth area of attention when discussing this offensive stance we are to take is that we be filled with the Holy Spirit.

> And be not drunk with wine, wherein is excess; but be filled with the Spirit. (verse 5:18)

We must never give ourselves over to other influences such as alcohol, drugs, hypnotism, or cultish religion that dull our own control. We must always stay in the place of control of our own will, understanding, and movement. If we are walking circumspectly and fulfilling the will of God, we must have an understanding, aggressive movement. In the place of other influences, we must be filled with (or under the full control and direction of) the Holy Spirit.

The sixth area of focus is praise and worship.

> Speaking to yourselves in psalms and hymns and spiritual songs, singing and making melody in your heart to the Lord. (verse 5:19)

James 1:2-4 tells us to react with joy when temptation comes.

> My brethren, count it all joy when ye fall into divers temptations; Knowing this, that the trying of your faith worketh patience. But let patience have her perfect work, that ye may be perfect and entire, wanting nothing

In his letter to the Romans, Paul made a similar statement when he talked about tribulation. Not only do we rejoice in the hope of the glory of God, but we "glory in tribulations also: knowing that tribulation worketh patience; And patience, experience; and experience, hope." (Romans 5:2-4)

From these verses, it is easy to see that these great apostles of the faith didn't count temptation and troubles as occasions for discouragement. Rather, temptation was an occasion for praising the Lord. Joy and rejoicing were their responses when Satan tried to get them down. They knew that they needed strength, and it is likely that they remembered that Nehemiah had said, "The joy of the Lord is your strength." (verse 8:10) When he and Silas were in the Philippian jail in Acts chapter sixteen, Paul proved that joy rather than discouragement was the better response to trouble. They had been beaten, imprisoned, and held in chains. At midnight, when everything was the darkest, they were singing and praising God. Through their praises, an earthquake delivered them from the jail. These apostles could rejoice and praise God through their troubles because they saw that the final result of all soulical temptation and physical tribulation is a stronger spiritual character. James claimed that the final result was "wanting nothing" (verse 1:4), and Paul said that it was having nothing to make us ashamed (Romans 5:5). These apostles saw that not only does the believer need to praise God during temptation and look for God to work out a stronger spiritual character, but they saw that the believer needs to stand on his own two feet, so to speak, during these temptations.

Paul called for Christians to put on the whole armor of God to be able to stand against temptation. (verse 6:11-14) James called for the believers to submit to God, resist the devil, and then draw near to God. (verse 4:7-8) How beautifully these apostles sandwiched the believers' fight against the devil between statements about living close to God. They both encouraged us to fight the devil from a place of protection in the Lord. We are to stand on our own two feet, but on ground that has been established by Christ.

Paul emphasized this point when he said, "Wherefore let him that thinketh he standeth take heed lest he fall." (I Corinthians 10:12) "There hath no temptation taken you but such as is common to man: but God is faithful, who will not suffer you to be tempted above that ye are able; but will with the temptation also make a way to escape, that ye may be able to bear it." (I Corinthians 10:13) If we try to stand alone, we will fall. But if we stand in Christ, we will always be able to match the temptations and have praise to utter during the conquest.

If Rule Number One of enduring temptation is to praise the Lord, then Rule Number Two is to get close to Jesus while fighting the devil. Peter and the author of Hebrews also agreed with this second rule. "The Lord knoweth how to deliver the godly out of temptations, and to reserve the unjust unto the day of judgment to be punished." (II Peter 2:9) "For we have not an high priest which cannot be touched with the feeling of our infirmities; but was in all points tempted like as we are, yet without sin. Let us therefore come boldly unto the throne of grace, that we may obtain mercy, and find grace to help in time of need." (Hebrews 4:15-16)

Troubles are a part of the walk of a believer. Paul reminded the Galatians that walking in the Spirit meant constantly encountering and overcoming temptation. "This I say then, Walk in the Spirit, and ye shall not fulfil the lust of the flesh. For the flesh lusteth against the Spirit, and the Spirit against the flesh: and these are contrary the one to the other: so that ye cannot do the things that ye would. But if ye be led of the Spirit, ye are not under the law." (Galatians 5:16-18)

James added a new "beatitude" -- that of enduring temptation. "Blessed is the man that endureth temptation: for when he is tried, he shall receive the crown of life, which the Lord hath promised to them that love him." (James 1:12)

Even Jesus was tempted.

And Jesus being full of the Holy Ghost

returned from Jordan, and was led by the Spirit into the wilderness, Being forty days tempted of the devil. And in those days he did eat nothing: and when they were ended, he afterward hungered…And when the devil had ended all the temptation, he departed from him for a season. And Jesus returned in the power of the Spirit into Galilee: and there went out a fame of him through all the region round about. (Luke 4:1-2, 13-14)

What a beautiful difference Luke describes in Jesus' life as a result of His enduring temptation, from being <u>filled</u> with the Holy Spirit to being <u>empowered</u> by the Holy Spirit. Having this kind of end result for overcoming temptation makes it easy to praise God and stand with Christ while the devil tempts. When we understand that while we are in the middle of spiritual warfare that we can praise God, we are able to draw ourselves into a place where we come out on the other side with a stronger stance, a purer life, and a closer relationship with Jesus. We can then rejoice and not be upset because we are in a trial -- not joy that we are in the struggle, but joy that there is a better prize set for us when we come to the other side.

Praising God is an absolute necessity to being an overcomer. Praise is an actual form of warfare. When we praise God, we establish a place for the presence of the Lord. "But thou art holy, O thou that inhabitest the praises of Israel." (Psalm 22:3) Joy is inherent in the presence of God. "Thou wilt shew me the path of life: in thy presence is fulness of joy; at thy right hand there are pleasures for evermore." (Psalm 16:11) Where the joy of the Lord is, there is strength. "Then he said unto them, Go your way, eat the fat, and drink the sweet, and send portions unto them for whom nothing is prepared: for this day is holy unto our Lord: neither be ye sorry; for the joy of the LORD is your strength." (Nehemiah 8:10) From the strength that we receive from the Lord as a result of the joy, we know that "I can do all things through Christ which strengtheneth me." (Philippians 4:13) Our praise establishes the presence, which brings the joy, which produces the strength with the end result that we are victorious in all things. Praise warfare is a very important key that we must have. With this key, we can go into spiritual warfare with a totally victorious attitude. Praise is not only the propelling force to get us through the battle; it also establishes strength in our lives during the conflict.

Second Chronicles chapter twenty tells the familiar story of Jehoshaphat. The armies of the enemies were approaching, and Israel was far outnumbered; so Jehoshaphat declared a fast and sought the Lord for His intervention. The Lord answered, "Ye shall not need to fight in this battle: set yourselves, stand ye still, and see the salvation of the LORD with you, O Judah and Jerusalem: fear not, nor be dismayed; to morrow go out against them: for the LORD will be with you." (verse 17) Then all the people of Israel worshipped the Lord. (verse 18)

God called them to the same revelation that He gave us in Ephesians chapter six concerning spiritual warfare. The verbs Paul uses are not verbs of struggle, but of standing in position with our authority, realizing that Christ has "spoiled principalities and powers, he made a shew of them openly" (Colossians 2:15) and now He is seated far above them (Ephesians 1:20-21) -- and, best of all, we are accompanying Him in that position of dominion (verse 2:6). God told Jehoshaphat to stand still because the battle was the Lord's; that is exactly what Paul was telling us in the book of Ephesians (verses 6:11, 14) -- stand still and accept the victory that has already been won for us.

Worship is an important element in bringing us into victorious spiritual warfare. Jehoshaphat "...appointed singers unto the LORD, and that should praise the beauty of holiness, as they went out before the army, and to say, Praise the LORD; for his mercy endureth for ever." (verse

21) Even though Jehoshaphat knew that praise and worship would be the important elements to win the victory, he did have his army dressed in battle array, ready for combat. Likewise, Paul tells us to "take on the whole armor of God." (verses 6:11, 13) We are not to act like there isn't a battle -- we get dressed for the battle even though we know that God will do the fighting.

> And when they began to sing and to praise, the LORD set ambushments against the children of Ammon, Moab, and mount Seir, which were come against Judah; and they were smitten. For the children of Ammon and Moab stood up against the inhabitants of mount Seir, utterly to slay and destroy them: and when they had made an end of the inhabitants of Seir, every one helped to destroy another. And when Judah came toward the watch tower in the wilderness, they looked unto the multitude, and, behold, they were dead bodies fallen to the earth, and none escaped. And when Jehoshaphat and his people came to take away the spoil of them, they found among them in abundance both riches with the dead bodies, and precious jewels, which they stripped off for themselves, more than they could carry away: and they were three days in gathering of the spoil, it was so much. And on the fourth day they assembled themselves in the valley of Berachah; for there they blessed the LORD: therefore the name of the same place was called, The valley of Berachah, unto this day. Then they returned, every man of Judah and Jerusalem, and Jehoshaphat in the forefront of them, to go again to Jerusalem with joy; for the LORD had made

them to rejoice over their enemies. And they came to Jerusalem with psalteries and harps and trumpets unto the house of the LORD. (verses 22-28)

James told us to "count it all joy," not because we are to have the struggle but because we will come out from the struggle stronger than when we went in. (verses 1:2-4) When Jehoshaphat's army went out to fight the battle, they did not have the three days worth of loot and booty in their hands that they eventually ended up with. They came into the battle with a genuine concern on their hearts. But they sought God until they finally came to the place that they could worship God, have faith in God, and draw nigh to God; then they used their praise to propel their spiritual weapons forward as they went into the battle. Instead of losing their houses, land, and families, they returned home with so much treasure that it took them three days to gather it all up. They came back better than when they went out to fight. James tells us that when we come to the temptation or trial, we must come to it with rejoicing because we know that on the other side we will be better off for having faced the conflict; Paul assures us that we will "not be ashamed." (Romans 5:1-5) Jehoshaphat's army came back full of rejoicing not only because their enemy had been defeated but also because they came back to Jerusalem with great wealth.

There is a victory that we will establish when we do warfare through praise. For Jehoshaphat there was a battle, there was a struggle, and there was warfare; however, he only had to stand and watch it happen! He simply observed the battle from his position of authority. Jehoshaphat came home that day as more than a conqueror. He did not have to fight the battle; he just reached out and took the reward from the battle.

Let me stress one important fact concerning Jehoshaphat's victory -- it was manifested through praise, but the praise was established on the covenant relationship that Israel had with God. Notice that before Jehoshaphat commissioned the praisers, he reviewed and re-affirmed that covenant. It was only after he knew for certain God's promise and commitment to be Israel's defender that he was ready to rejoice. After purifying himself and his nation, Jehoshaphat was assured that they were in the right spiritual relationship to expect those covenant benefits. At that point, he was so full of faith that he called the army's accompanying band to begin to play the victor's march that they normally reserved for the march home after a victorious campaign. To Jehoshaphat, the victory had already been won so he didn't have to wait to see the final score; he could sing the triumphant song in advance! The power of his praise was based on the power of his faith in his covenant. So it is with us -- we must be grounded in the foundational truths Paul is explaining if we are to see victory.

When Jehoshaphat put the praise singers in the front of the army, they were not equipped with the shields, swords, helmets, and breastplates. They went forth as a choir. Before we get to the place of "finally, my brethren" and take up the shield, sword, helmet, and breastplate, we must come into praise, singing, and worship. Perhaps there is some symbolism in the fact that Moses numbered the warriors from twenty years old (Numbers 1:3), but he numbered the Levites, the priestly tribe, from one month old (Numbers 3:28). I think that this census tells us that we are to begin to serve in our worship relationship and in our priestly role the moment we are born again. The warrior position is something that we grow into, but we are to begin our role of the worshipping and praising immediately.

The power of a song or a jingle is tremendous. It has the ability to get into our subconscious mind and demand to be heard over and over and over. We use the term "earworm" to refer to these little songs that we just can't get out of our heads. I understand that Walt Disney's "It's a Small World" is considered to be the most difficult earworm to overcome. It is because of this kind of overwhelming force that jingles and songs can have that companies are willing to spend millions of dollars to get the right jingle to advertise their products. God wants to use exactly the same principle to get His victorious Word inside us through psalms, hymns, and spiritual songs. The scripture tells us to meditate on the Word -- a term that means mutter it over and over and repeat it inside ourselves. (Psalm 1:2)

The Holy Spirit tells us to sing and make melody in our hearts. Through that melody, the Word of God will get inside us to the point that we begin to bubble and churn with its truth. The words that go with that melody are being reinforced over and over, making us stronger warriors. This use of psalms, hymns, and spiritual songs is actually one way of redeeming the time -- we may not always be sitting down reading the Bible, but the Word of God is bubbling on the inside of us because that melody keeps coming up.

One other important truth to note is that our praise and worship are actually to be oriented to one another. Although some versions read, "speaking to yourselves" leaving the implication that this praise is to be for personal edification, many translations give a more literal rendition of "speaking to one another" (verse 5:19 NKJV) helping us to see that the edification is actually a corporate experience. Though we can encourage ourselves in the Lord through our positive praise, we are also called to bring encouragement to the Body of Christ by ministering positive praise to our brothers and sisters. This is why the author of Hebrews insisted that we not forsake assembling as a body for worship, especially as the evil day is approaching. (verse 10:25)

Point seven may not seem aggressive at first, but it is -- being thankful. (verse 5:20) Giving thanks is a very powerful tool. Jesus healed ten lepers, but the Bible says that only one was made whole because he came back to give thanks. (Luke 17:11-19) The Bible says that the other nine were healed, but it gives us no indication that the parts of their bodies that had been eaten away by the leprosy were ever restored. If they had already lost earlobes to the leprosy, when they were healed there was no more leprosy, but the earlobes would still be missing. However, the one who came back and gave thanks was made whole. This means that he received a creative miracle in his body and his missing earlobes grew back.

A dear friend of mine served as director of Nepal Leprosy Fellowship for more than fifty years. Among all the other things that I learned from this saint of God was one lesson that really made this story of the ten lepers come alive. She explained that the mission had two objectives -- to heal the patients and to reconstruct their disfigured bodies. I obviously understood the significance of the first objective, but had never really considered the importance of the second thrust. Of course, I had been around enough lepers in my mission travels to know how unsettling it is to see the disfigured victims on the train or on the street. Even when the victim has been cured and is no longer contagious and is in no way a threat to society, the nubs he has for fingers, the missing earlobes, and the hole in the front of his face where a nose should be are enough to make everyone give him a wide perimeter. For these patients to be able to be accepted back into their homes and re-integrated into society, it is just as important that their deformities be dealt with as it is for their contagious conditions to be treated. Without reconstructive plastic surgery, these victims are doomed to the same miserable lives as outcasts that they had previously known. So it was with nine of the men who came to Jesus that day; they may have received certification from the priests that they were cured, but they would not be welcomed back by their wives, families, or employers. Only one -- the thankful one who was made whole -- was able to find welcoming arms waiting for him when he made his way back to his village.

God will do so much for every Christian, but it seems that He does more for those who are thankful. When we get to the point of thanking God for what we do have rather than grumbling over what we do not have, we will find out how much more He is willing to bless us.

Submission

At verse twenty-one, Paul changed from one emphasis to another in the middle of the lengthy sentence that began in verse eighteen. Here, he changed his focus from aggressive movement to interpersonal relationships. He introduced the general arena of human inter-workings by giving us a cross-the-board generalization: submit to one another.

> Submitting yourselves one to another in the fear of God.

We have to be soldiers in the army under a chain of authority. Matthew 8:5-10 tells the story of the centurion who knew that things happened when he gave the command because he was a man under authority. If we are not under authority, we cannot necessarily believe that things will happen when we speak. If we are submitted to authority, when we speak, the authorities under us move because they are responding not only our authority but also to the authority above us. The reason the centurion could have faith was because he was under authority.

Next, Paul turned to some very practical where-the-rubber-meets-the-road issues concerning submission. It may be easy for us as believers to live in good harmony with our fellow church members whom we see only a couple hours one day each week, but to really know if we can apply the principles of submission, we have to take them into the crucible of where we live seven days a week -- the family -- and where we live forty hours each week -- the workplace.

When the apostle began to discuss submission, he focused on our family and business relationships. These areas must be in order before we can begin spiritual warfare. If we don't have harmony in our family and the right relationship in our business, we are not going to be able to go out and fight on the front line against an opposing enemy. If we can't have harmony with those we call friends, we certainly cannot have victory against our enemies. Dick Eastman, President of Every Home for Christ, once observed that the ultimate spiritual maturity and personal fulfillment in life for the followers of Jesus is best taught, tempered, and tested in God's laboratory of life -- the family.

Paul's first area of admonition is to the wives who are told to submit themselves to their husbands.

> Wives, submit yourselves unto your own husbands, as unto the Lord. (verse 5:22)

Please make certain that you understand that the verse is talking about husbands and wives. It does not say, "Women, submit yourselves to all men," which is exactly the way many people interpret New Testament relationships. The submission Paul is talking about is the relationship within the home; it is not genetic or chromosomal. It is not a situation where a woman cannot teach and have men sit under her teaching. It is not a situation where a woman cannot be a pastor and have men sit under her pastoral leadership. In the Body of Christ, women are not on a second status below men. It is within the individual home that the wife submits to her own husband. In the home, someone has to make the final decision. This kind of recognized order brings us to a place of security in the home because we know that there is one person who is in charge. Paul puts the word "own" in the verse for clear distinction. Paul does not intend that a woman submit herself to somebody else's husband. A husband only has authority over his own wife.

Wives are told to submit to their own husbands "as to the Lord." There is a different kind of submission that you have to the Lord than the kind of submission that you have to a slave driver. Many men have taken this verse thinking they could be "Simon Legree" from Uncle Tom's Cabin. We do not submit ourselves to the Lord out of fear thinking that He is going to beat us up if we don't please Him. We submit ourselves to the Lord in response to the love He has poured into us. Jesus went to the cross and died for us; therefore, we can't help but submit to Him. If He loves us that much, He must have our best interests in mind, and we cannot help but yield to Him. That is the kind of submission Paul is asking the women to move into in relationship to their husbands.

Paul's second focus is on the husbands who are told to treat their wives like the Lord treats the church.

> For the husband is the head of the wife,
> even as Christ is the head of the church:
> and he is the saviour of the body. (verse 5:23)

The husband is then shocked into the realization that he must be in the same position that Jesus is in. Jesus doesn't go around bossing and barking at the church. Jesus is the savior to the church. He gave Himself to save the church. That is the kind of relationship that a wife should expect in a Christian husband. If she is going to submit to him, she has the right to expect him to be a giver and provider for her just as Christ is to the church.

Christ gave Himself over to abuse so that He could sanctify His Bride and bring her to Himself holy and without spot or blemish. He paid everything so that He could give it all to His Bride. Jesus spared no expense so that the church could be the most beautiful bride that she could be. (verses 5:25-27) This kind of love is what is expected from every Christian husband who is preparing for spiritual warfare.

Notice the overwhelming emphasis Paul places on the husband's role in the home. In verse thirty-three, Paul says, "Let...the wife see that she reverence her husband." This is his second sentence in relationship to the wife -- the first sentence and the last sentence of this section focus on the wife, but the meat in the middle of the sandwich -- verses twenty-three through the middle of verse thirty-three -- zero in on the husband's responsibility. The fact that the wife gets one and a half verses and the husband gets ten and a half verses should tell us something -- the husband is to be the head of the house and he must take on a tremendous responsibility of being in the leadership so that the wife has a very simple role of respecting him in that leadership position. She respects him because of who he is, how much he has given himself to her, and how sincere and dedicated he is. She can submit herself to him because he is treating her like the Lord treats the church. This line of authority in the home provides the foundation necessary for exercising supernatural authority in spiritual warfare.

The children are told to obey their parents in Paul's third area of focus.

> Children, obey your parents in the Lord: for
> this is right. (verse 6:1)

The Bible says that we must honor our father and mother in order for our days on the earth to be long and fulfilling. (Exodus 20:12, Deuteronomy 5:16)   Paul prophesied that in the last days children would be disobedient to parents (Romans 1:30, II Timothy 3:2); we can see this passage proven by observing the increase in youthful deaths resulting from gang activity, drug overdoses, sexually transmitted disease, suicide, and accidents resulting from rebellious actions such as driving under the influence of drugs or alcohol or recklessness and excessive speeding. Every time a young person dies as a result of any of these causes, he again proves the validity of the scripture's command that he should have honored his parents and obeyed their instructions. Instead, he has allowed the enemy to direct his life and eventually take it from him.

The fourth area Paul addresses is the role of the father with his children.

> And, ye fathers, provoke not your children
> to wrath: but bring them up in the nurture
> and admonition of the Lord. (verse 6:4)

It is interesting that Paul did not say, "Parents, do not provoke your children to wrath." All the weight is put on the fathers. This is exactly the same thing we discussed earlier regarding the husband's relationship to his wife. The father is the one who has to take the responsibility in the home.

A minister was trying to explain to me how that we need a fearful respect of God by paralleling his experience as a child who always obeyed his father for fear of being punished; eventually, I interrupted him saying that I couldn't relate to his story because of my own experience as a child. I understood the incredible love my parents had for me and I always wanted to respect and obey them out of a concern for disappointing them. I also had such a respect and admiration for them that I wanted to do everything possible to grow up to be like them. When the pastor heard this testimony, he was shocked and exclaimed that I must be the only one in the world with this experience. I somehow doubt that I'm the only one, but I am sure that I am in the minority. Maybe most of us haven't had this kind of positive relationship with our earthly fathers, but this is exactly the kind of relationship we can -- in fact, must -- have with our heavenly Father. And when we do, it will totally change our perspective and experience as Christians.

When he was leading the children of Israel through the Sinai Desert toward the Promised Land, God instructed Moses to strike the rock so that water could be provided for them. (Exodus 17:6) Later, when they came to another place where there was no water, God instructed Moses to speak to the rock. (Numbers 20:8) Perhaps out of anger toward the grumbling Israelites or perhaps out of lack of sensitivity to cautiously follow God's directions, Moses again struck the rock. He had done this before and water gushed out, but God wanted to lead the Israelites into another realm of faith by simply speaking to the rock this time. First Corinthians 10:4 tells us that the rock in the desert was a picture of Christ Jesus. The first time we come to Jesus, it is through the cross where He was struck. After that initial encounter, we simply come to Him and ask; then out of Him flows all the mercy and grace we need. Because Moses destroyed the object lesson God had designed in the rock, he was forbidden to enter into the Promised Land (Numbers 20:12) -- even though he had struggled for eighty years to get there.

Paul tells us in this passage that the family is a mystery of Christ and the church. (verse 5:32) When a Christian marriage is broken up, it destroys the symbol God has set up. Jesus taught us that our relationship with God is like a child with his father. He said that if we ask our earthly father for something we expect to receive it from him and how much more can we expect to receive good things from our heavenly Father. (Matthew 7:9-11) Paul spoke about our relationship to God saying that out of our spirit man we would cry, "Daddy, God." (Romans 8:15, Galatians 4:6) Yet today, we live in a world where the father-son relationship is almost totally destroyed. When I have tried to talk to some people about the goodness of their heavenly Father, I have had them look back at me and say, "That does not compute for me because my father did not love me." Some do not even know who their earthly fathers are.

We live in a day when the world has done exactly as Moses did -- they have struck the rock instead of speaking to it, destroying the symbol that God has put in the earth. I don't believe that God is going to be any more lenient with us than He was with Moses. Moses missed his Promised Land because he destroyed a symbol, and I believe we are a generation that is missing our Promised Land because we have destroyed God's symbols in our homes. We need to keep the family together. A husband needs to love his wife as Christ loved the church. A father has to love his children and not provoke them to anger but to bring them up in the nature and in admonition of the Lord. When our homes are weak or even destroyed, we have defeated ourselves on the home front. We must turn our homes back to proper spiritual order if we expect to succeed when we venture into spiritual warfare.

In his fifth and sixth points, Paul went beyond the home and talked about our business relationships. He told slaves to be obedient to their masters.

Servants, be obedient to them that are your

masters according to the flesh, with fear and trembling, in singleness of your heart, as unto Christ; Not with eyeservice, as menpleasers; but as the servants of Christ, doing the will of God from the heart; With good will doing service, as to the Lord, and not to men: Knowing that whatsoever good thing any man doeth, the same shall he receive of the Lord, whether he be bond or free. (verses 6:5-8)

Then he addressed the masters, telling them to treat their servants fairly.

And, ye masters, do the same things unto them, forbearing threatening: knowing that your Master also is in heaven; neither is there respect of persons with him. (verse 6:9)

In our business and work relationships we can't cheat or default our boss because we really don't work for him -- we actually work for God. The same thing is true with the boss -- he must realize that those who work under him are not really his employees; they belong to God. Therefore, he should treat them like they are God's property, acknowledging that He has allowed them to serve a human master because that human employer is answerable to God. In everything we do, we do it as unto the Lord, doing the will of God from the heart.

The truths of spiritual warfare are not for just supernatural conflict; they must show in our relationships with the people around us. It is when we have proper relationships with our husbands, our wives, our kids, our parents, our employers, and our employees that we are finally in the authority alignment to begin preparing for spiritual warfare. We are finally ready for the "finally, my brethren" of verse ten.

Before Paul lets us venture into spiritual warfare, he insisted that our new creation qualities be of sufficient substance and that they are practical and applicable within our homes and our businesses. Paul moved directly from our home and business relationships into spiritual warfare. We sometimes want to divorce ourselves from the practical things, thinking we are doing great at spiritual warfare and that it doesn't matter what kind of mess we have at our homes or how out of order the workplace is. We may think that we can divorce our practical living from our spiritual warfare, but the truth is that we can't fight our husband or our wife or our boss or our employees -- and the devil all at the same time. We must have harmony in our homes and workplaces. We must stop fighting flesh and blood in order to come into proper relationship and proper love in our home and business. Then -- and only then -- can we be victorious in spiritual warfare.

When we realize that we can't fight with our spouses and the devil at the same time, it brings new meaning to the passage about not wrestling with flesh and blood but with principalities.

After Having Eaten The Baby

At the end of a morning service, I told the congregation that I was going to minister to them in the evening service on "After Having Eaten the Baby." After meditating all afternoon about what they thought they were going to hear when they came back to the service, there were many varied ideas. Some recalled the Old Testament story of the Samaritan city under siege by the Syrians. The enemy had surrounded the city and set up blockades so that no supplies could get to the people. The people were starving to the point that one woman actually ate her own child. (II Kings 6:28-29) Others came to the service anticipating that I was going to tell them the story of a black-robed Satanists who had participated in some kind of human sacrifice and had actually eaten human flesh in some kind of cannibalistic mock of the holy communion. Perhaps I was going to tell of a deliverance of one of these Satanic high priests who came to Jesus after having eaten a baby. Some thought I was going to tell the story of aboriginal cannibals wearing nothing but war paint and blood splattered across their faces as they gorged on the feast of their conquered foe.

I surprised them all when I opened my Bible to the book of Ephesians and read from chapter six, "Wherefore take unto you the whole armour of God, that ye may be able to withstand in the evil day, and having done all, to stand. Stand therefore, having your loins girt about with truth, and having on the breastplate of righteousness..." (verses 6:13-14) Of course, everybody wanted to know what that had to do with eating babies. I told them that they had only heard half of my sentence. My sentence actually says, "After having eaten, the baby threw his bowl to the floor."

The Grammar

The problem with most interpretations of this passage of scripture is that we neglect the commas. When we leave out the commas or put the commas in the wrong place, we do just as much violation to this sentence from the Word of God as the congregation had done to the sentence about the baby's eating. We get a totally different meaning by misplacing the commas. Most often, we read Ephesians 6:13-14 with total disregard of how it was written. We interpret it as: "Having done everything we know how to do and we have run out of all the tricks of the trade -- then, when there is nothing else to do, we just staunchly keep on keeping on." That may be a good philosophy, but that is not what the scripture is saying. This scripture is telling us to put on the armor of God so we can do two things: to withstand and to stand.

Notice that there are a couple commas in this sentence. One comes after the word "day" and the other comes between the words "all" and "to." The commas indicate to us that there is a parenthetical phrase that has been added into the sentence. We can remove the parenthetical phrase, and the sentence has exactly the same meaning. There is a little clarification given by having put the parenthetical phrase in, but the clarification is not necessary to convey the intended meaning of the sentence.

In the sentence "The teacher, not the students, is in charge of the class," the phrase "not the students" is a parenthetical phrase which is added in. It certainly clarifies the thought, but it is not necessary for the sentence to have meaning.

Taking the parenthetical phrase out of this verse gives us the basic meaning of the text. Without the added information the sentence becomes easier to read, and we can see exactly what Paul is saying to us. The verse would then say, "Therefore, take up the whole armor of God that you may be able to withstand in the evil day…and to stand." This is the basic meaning of what Paul is saying here. The next sentence (which we usually blend into this thought) is actually a separate thought. Notice that there is a period that indicates a break in the flow between verse thirteen and verse fourteen. With this understanding, it is clear that Paul is telling us to take up the whole armor of God for two purposes: that in the evil day we can withstand and we can stand.

The parenthetical phrase that we dropped out of verse thirteen reads, "having done all." Some translations include the alternate wording "having overcome all" leaving the impression that we will be able to stand after we have defeated all our obstacles. Such a reading can be misleading in that it implies that we are the ones doing the overcoming when, in fact, it was Jesus Christ who won the victory through His crucifixion and resurrection. It seems more in keeping with the overall theme of the passage to keep the traditional reading, "having done all." Once we have touched all the bases, we finally come to the point of putting on our armor and taking our victorious stance. I am convinced that Paul was telling us that these foundational steps that he has enumerated in the first five and a half chapters of his letter must be completed before we can be assured of standing. The picture Paul is going to paint concerning spiritual warfare is far beyond what most Christians ever imagine or experience. The reason they drag from Sunday to Sunday and are always defeated, not knowing who is going to win -- them or the devil -- is that they have failed in implementing these foundational points.

We fail to see many of the fundamental truths of this passage because we have overlooked the grammar. We miss the adverb "finally." We ignore the plural nature of the noun "brethren." We overlook the punctuation in the passage, failing to recognize how the commas and the period set off a parenthetical phrase and break the thought into two separate sentences. But worse of all, we ignore the verbs which carry the meaning of the passage.

Standing vs. Wrestling

> Finally, my brethren, be strong in the Lord, and in the power of his might. Put on the whole armour of God, that ye may be able to stand against the wiles of the devil. (verses 6:10-11)

I want you to notice that Paul said that he wanted us to be able to stand. He did not tell us to get down and tumble with the enemy. "Stand" is the key word in this verse. We call this a spiritual warfare passage, but it really ought to be labeled a "spiritual standing" passage. Paul really does not talk about waging war. He is talking about standing.

> For we wrestle not against flesh and blood, but against principalities, against powers, against the rulers of the darkness of this world, against spiritual wickedness in high places. Wherefore take unto you the whole armour of God, that ye may be able to withstand in the evil day, and having done all, to stand. (verses 6:12-13)

If we have done all the things we have discussed up to this point, we will be able to stand. If we come into a spiritual conflict having done these things, we can put on the armor of God and be certain that we are going to be able to stand unmovable.

Paul used two different analogies here. He mixed his metaphors in this passage, something that he does at other points in his writings as well. In II Timothy 2:3-6, he shifted from a soldier image to an athletic image, and finally to a farming image in just four little verses. In the passage we are studying in Ephesians, the word "wrestle" comes from the sports or athletic arena. Wrestling is not something done on the battlefield; it is a form of entertainment. When we go to the battlefield we don't wrestle -- you do warfare. Paul said, "We don't wrestle against flesh and blood." We have all seen pictures of the famous Greek statue of the discus thrower who is clad only in his discus. The Greeks had no embarrassment with the human body. They felt that it was a creation of the gods and that it was beautiful. Therefore, at the time of Paul's writing, these sports events occurred in the nude because they didn't want any hindrance in their movements. In fact, the Greek word for "gymnasium" literally means, "nude training." The same is true today. We don't go out to play tennis in a three-piece suit and top hat. We wear the briefest of sports apparel because we know that any added weight can hold us back. In fact, I had friends on the college swim team who shaved their heads and their whole bodies because they knew that even a hair would give resistance and slow them down -- and this was in the 1970s when all the guys were wearing shoulder-length hair!

It is in order to confront this naked opponent, Paul tells us to put on the armor of God. Just imagine these principalities and wicked spiritual creatures in high places gathered together in their corner of the ring ready to have a wrestling match with the Christian, expecting him to come into the ring in his "birthday suit." The door opens from the other changing room and out comes the Christian dressed in a girdle, a breastplate, a helmet, shoes, a sword, and a shield. When the demons see a fully armored warrior walking out, you can imagine how they have to regroup. Just guess who will win such a wrestling match. Dr. Lester Sumrall once said it this way, "When you appear with all of heaven's gear on, every devil in hell recognizes it."

In Colossians 2:15, Paul expanded the discussion of the devil's nakedness. "And having spoiled principalities and powers, he made a shew of them openly, triumphing over them in it." The literal meaning of "spoiled" is "stripped him naked." The verse is actually rendered this way in some modern translations, vividly reiterating the scene being set here. The imagery behind this wording comes from the ancient practice of defrocking the kings and other political and military leaders of conquered nations. When those defeated enemies were brought back from the battle, they were totally humiliated by being marched through the streets naked -- no longer with royal robes or regalia of rank. Through the wording here, Paul painted a vivid picture to awaken his reader to the fact that the opponent against whom we are to stand is an already defeated foe.

Think about any wrestling match you have ever watched. How much time is spent standing up? Almost none of it! The two opponents start in a locked position; but as soon as the whistle blows, one of them knocks the other to the floor, and they spend their time tumbling and tossing on the floor until one is able to pin the other down and hold his shoulders to the mat for the ten count. Wrestling matches are not held standing up. But Paul told us time and again that our position is not tumbling nip and tuck on the floor. Our position is to stand. We are told to put on the armor of God so that we will be able to stand. Verse fourteen repeats, "Stand, therefore." Our position is not a wrestling position of tumbling on the floor, but it is a standing position. Why is it that we can walk into spiritual conflict and have such a position of authority? If we take care of these first five and a half chapters of instructions -- you might call them our layers of underwear -- we can put on salvation, knowledge, truth, etc. and walk boldly into the face of whatever the devil tries to do. We will recognize that the devil's tactics are tricks and lies, and we can withstand them and we keep on standing.

Paul says that we may be buffeted when the enemy attacks. "There was given to me a thorn in the flesh, the messenger of Satan to buffet me." (II Corinthians 12:7) When such literal attacks come, we have to add a second line of defense -- withstanding as well as standing. Withstanding carries a slightly different meaning from standing. When we stand against the enemy, we are simply exerting our authority; however, when we withstand the enemy, we may be actually taking some blows in the process. To understand this concept, let's take a quick look at a parable that Jesus told about withstanding. In his story about the houses which the wise man and the foolish man built, we read, "And the rain descended, and the floods came, and the winds blew, and beat upon that house; and it fell not: for it was founded upon a rock." (Matthew 7:25, also Luke 6:48) Notice that the house actually endured the hollowing winds and the crashing waves. Although there is a difference between standing and withstanding in terms of actually taking a few punches along the way, the end result is the same -- we wind up standing rather than falling because we are anchored into the solid rock of faith. The rock is a foundation that the enemy cannot topple, "And I say also unto thee, That thou art Peter, and upon this rock I will build my church; and the gates of hell shall not prevail against it." (Matthew 16:18) Faith is a shield that the enemy cannot penetrate, "Above all, taking the shield of faith, wherewith ye shall be able to quench all the fiery darts of the wicked." (Ephesians 6:16)

This message seems to be the focus of his second letter to the Corinthians. When Paul wrote this letter, he had a specific message that he wanted to communicate. He spelled it out fairly directly in verses three through seven of the first chapter -- in every difficulty, we are comforted by God so that we can become comforters to others. The problem that he was addressing in this letter is the same one that is dealt with in the book of Job -- why do bad things happen to good men? Paul was certainly a good man, but he certainly had a lot of bad things happening in his life. Several times in this letter, he lists the things he had to endure for the gospel's sake. (verses 2:4, 4:8-12, 6:4-5, 11:23-28, 12:7-10, 15) These lists of attacks make us realize how easy we actually have it when we confront our little obstacles. However, we are amazed when Paul sums up his trials as "light affliction." (verse 4:17) He could say such an unthinkable thing because the real issue he was dealing with wasn't, "How come?" Instead, his mind was set on the question, "How to overcome?" In chapter six, he presented a sequence of phrases that depict the problems he has faced, the approach he took to dealing with them, and the results he obtained.

> But in all things approving ourselves as the ministers of God, in much patience, in afflictions, in necessities, in distresses, In stripes, in imprisonments, in tumults, in labours, in watchings, in fastings; By pureness, by knowledge, by longsuffering, by kindness, by the Holy Ghost, by love unfeigned, By the word of truth, by the power of God, by the armour of righteousness on the right hand and on the left, By honour and dishonour, by evil report and good report: as deceivers, and yet true; As unknown, and yet well known; as dying, and, behold, we live; as chastened, and not killed; As sorrowful, yet alway rejoicing; as poor, yet making many rich; as having nothing, and yet possessing all things. (verses 4-10)

He listed his persecutions (the problem) as "in" in verses four and five. The ways he overcame them (the approach) are listed as "by" in verses six, seven, and eight. The results of his defense (the result) are listed as "by" -- a different preposition in Greek -- in verses nine and ten. Interestingly, the approaches he used in his conflict are not the ones that we generally would list as our weapons for spiritual warfare; however, he called them his "weapons of righteousness on the right hand and on the left." (verse 4:7, MKJV)

Paul used this same word for weapons or armament in two different places in the book of Romans. We find it translated as "instruments" in Romans 6:13, "Neither yield ye your members as instruments of unrighteousness unto sin: but yield yourselves unto God, as those that are alive from the dead, and your members as instruments of righteousness unto God." In Romans 13:12, it is translated as "armor," "The night is far spent, the day is at hand: let us therefore cast off the works of darkness, and let us put on the armour of light." From the context, we can see that weapons are actual implications of the godly qualities of light and righteousness. In other words, Paul's power to overcome was not the "spiritual warfare" we might think of as screaming at the top one's lungs, rebuking the devil in tongues. Instead, his victory came through using the godly man's arsenal of righteous qualities.

Even though he described himself as suffering serious blows, he always seemed to bounce back victoriously. He was like the good man described in Proverbs 24:16 who, even if he falls seven times, always gets up again. The roly-poly toys we know as weebles can help us understand the powerful spiritual truth that dominated Paul's life. We've all enjoyed the amazement of "socking" the punch toy as hard as we can and watching it plop all the way to the floor -- only to immediately bounce back totally erect. The lesson -- as we all already know -- is "Weebles wobble, but they don't fall down." When we learn to use the total arsenal that God has provided for us, we'll soon be able to show forth that same resilience in our lives -- no matter how much we may wobble, we'll always bounce back! Because Paul had become a weeble for God, he was able to say in chapter ten verses three through five that the weapons of his warfare were not carnal but mighty through God to the pulling down of strongholds. That's why he could say in chapter two verse fourteen that God always caused him to triumph. This was the grace that he had to deal with the thorn in the flesh and Satan's messenger -- the "Timex watch grace" to take the licking and keep on ticking. (verse 12:9)

Another side note to this passage is that Paul described having the weaponry in each hand. It seems that the significance of this concept might go back to the time of the rebuilding of the wall around Jerusalem under Nehemiah's direction. In Nehemiah 4:17, we read, "They which builded on the wall, and they that bare burdens, with those that laded, every one with one of his hands wrought in the work, and with the other hand held a weapon." These were two-fisted warriors who were slapping mortar on wall with a trawl in one hand and threatening their enemies with a sword with the other. Building the wall was a passive form of defense while yielding a sword was an active form of defense. In this approach, we see a great lesson for all believers -- build yourself up in your faith as a passive resistance to the enemy's attacks while also aggressively challenging him every time he shows up!

The Apostle John amens this truth when he says that we can actually become immune to the effects of the work of the enemy, "We know that whosoever is born of God sinneth not; but he that is begotten of God keepeth himself, and that wicked one toucheth him not." (I John 5:18)

Several years ago, I went to see the prehistoric pagan shrine Stonehenge in England on June 21, the only day of the year that the British government grants permission for people to go inside the fence surrounding the monoliths. The sun-worship cults demanded their religious rights and convinced the government to open the gates on this one day so they could do their ceremonies on this particular day when the sun rises over the central altar. As I was touring the site, one of the sun worshipers stood up and began threatening our group because he felt that we were desecrating the sun worshiper's event by talking. One of the guys in our group -- a huge hunk of a man -- walked around to the man making all the threats and started cracking his knuckles as if he were ready for a fight. The sun worshiper whimpered and went back to his devilish chants trying to pretend that we weren't there. This big hunk of a man never had to get down and tumble on the ground. Our "hero" never had to do anything physical to anybody. He just walked toward our opponent and stood there. His massive presence demonstrated that he was in authority. When he cracked his knuckles, he sent out such a strong message that the challenger simply left us alone.

The sun worshiper knew that he had met more than his match. Our friend defeated the enemy the same way Jesus did Satan during His temptation when He stood firm on His authority -- in Jesus' case, the Word of God -- until the devil left Him. Imagine how much more authoritatively we can stand now that we have the New Testament to add to the Old Testament authority on which Jesus stood.

Paul was telling us that we Christians can go into spiritual warfare with confidence that we will not fail. If we have done everything to properly prepare, we can walk onto the battlefield and stand our ground. We don't have to get down and roll on the mat with the devil. We can walk in the kind of authority that makes the devil shiver.

If we submit ourselves to God and resist the devil, the enemy has to flee. (James 4:7) The devil doesn't tumble around on the floor with us and maybe win one round and get in a couple of good blows -- instead, he gets up and runs! He may try to growl, but he cannot stand against us because we are walking in authority. However, we cannot get that authority by just starting in chapter six verse ten. We get that authority by starting in chapter one verse one and making sure that we have on all our layers of underwear. Then we can put on our spiritual armament and we walk out on the battlefield, able to stand. Having done everything, we stand.

When my three sons were children, I would wrestle with them. They would grab me around my legs and begin jerking and pulling. Eventually I would lie down for them so that we could roll and tumble a little bit. That would make the boys feel more like my equal. Paul declared that if we have this armor on, we will not be on the floor with the devil. We will be able to stand. He is not our equal. We can stand firmly if we want to. It is only when we lie down willingly (perhaps through ignorance of our authority) that he can get us to the floor.

Standing without giving up is what putting on the armor of God is all about. The Word of God is replete with admonitions about standing:

We stand in faith. (Romans 5:2, I Corinthians 16:13, II Corinthians 1:24)

We are instructed to stand in our divine election. (Romans 9:11)

We must stand in God's ability. (Romans 14:4)

We can stand in the power of God. (I Corinthians 2:5)

We are admonished to stand in the gospel. (I Corinthians 15:1)

We are told to stand in the liberty that Christ has given us. (Galatians 5:1)

We are required to stand in one spirit. (Philippians 1:27)

We can only stand in the Lord. (Philippians 4:1, I Thessalonians 3:8)

We are able to stand in the Word of God. (II Thessalonians 2:15)

We will stand in the will of God by intercessory prayer. (Colossians 4:12)

We victoriously stand by the grace of God. (I Peter 5:12)

We triumphantly stand in the day of wrath. (Revelation 6:17)

We must learn to stand against the wiles of the devil. (Ephesians 6:11)

Pulling Down Strongholds

Let's look at another passage that demonstrates our area of spiritual dominion.

> For though we walk in the flesh, we do not war after the flesh: (For the weapons of our warfare are not carnal, but mighty through God to the pulling down of strong holds;) Casting down imaginations, and every high thing that exalteth itself against the knowledge of God, and bringing into captivity every thought to the obedience of Christ. (II Corinthians 10:3-5)

For many years when I read this passage, I thought that the things that exalt themselves against the knowledge of God were ideas like atheism that says there is no God or Hinduism that says that Vishnu, Krishna, Ganesh, or any one of the other millions of their deities is God, or Buddhism that claims Gautama to be divine, or even New Age that tells us that we all are gods. Then one day, the Holy Spirit prompted me to realize that even though I rejected all these pagan beliefs that I still harbored thoughts that exalted themselves against God. When I challenged Him as to how it was possible that I could possibly have such thoughts, He questioned me as to what I know about God. I responded that He is Jehovah Rapha, the God who heals all my diseases. The Holy Spirit then quickened to me the reality that any time I thought that my healing was in the medicine cabinet, a doctor's office, or a hospital that I was actually entertaining a thought that was exalting itself against what I really knew about God. He then asked me what else I knew about God. This time, I answered that I knew Him to be Jehovah Jireh, the God who provides all my needs according to His riches in glory. Again He challenged me that every time I thought that my provision was in a bank loan, a higher credit card limit, working extra hours, or asking the boss for a raise that I was again entertaining thoughts that exalted themselves against the true knowledge of God. By the time that this little soul-searching session had taken me through several more truths about the Lord, I began to understand what this passage is really saying. It is a truth that can and must be applied to every area of our lives. Our weapons are strong enough to destroy the arguments against the knowledge of God. There are many areas of truth that we should know about God; however, for some reason, we don't comprehend and live in them because there is an idea that has gotten into our heads that keeps the true knowledge of God from getting inside of us. We know that God exists, but we fail to attain the true knowledge of who God is and what God does.

God is Jehovah Tsidkenu, which means that He is the God of our righteousness. The day that Jesus came into our lives, His righteousness came into us. However, the devil will come to each and every one of us with accusations to combat any awareness we have of this righteousness. If we open ourselves to these accusations, just like David's stone found that tiny eyehole in Goliath' armor, the devil will aim for this vulnerable spot. If that lie penetrates into our minds and we agree with it, he begins to build a stronghold against the knowledge of God's righteousness within us.

God is also Jehovah Rapha -- the God who heals all of our diseases -- but the devil wants to plant lies inside us saying that our ailment is either too big for God to heal or too insignificant for Him to notice. The truth is that God is just as willing to heal the little aches and pains as He is to heal major diseases. He is just as able to heal the most dreaded plague as He is to cure a minor ailment.

We can go through all the redemptive names and qualities of God to learn what we should be thinking about God. Any time we allow thoughts contrary to these truths into our hearts, we have permitted the enemy to use his deceit to begin a stronghold in our minds.

When we look at the armor, notice the extremely significant relationship that keeps occurring. It always comes back to our mind, our voice, and our spirit man -- these are the areas where the devil wants to exert his authority: in our minds, our thinking, and our hearing and speaking.

We have a girdle of truth because truth works in the area of the mind and voice. Our feet are prepared with the gospel of peace; "gospel" also means "good news," and it relates to our minds and voices. Our shield is one of faith that comes by hearing of the Word (Romans 10:17); faith works in the area of our voice when we speak the word of faith (Romans 10:8). Our offensive stance is taken in prayer and relates to our mind, voice, and spirit. The sword that the apostle admonishes us to take hold of is the Word of God, but not just a general word. The Greek term used here is *rhema*, which means the specific word on a topic -- not *logos*, which means the general concept behind the topic. When Jesus taught us about the word that was sown in the fields with uncertain results -- some was eaten by ravens, some was choked out by thorns, some was scorched by the sun, and only part was productive -- He used the term *logos*. (Mark 4:14) However, when the term *rhema* is used, the context is always in reference to the word that does not return until it accomplishes the purpose unto which it was sent. (Matthew 4:4, Luke 5:5, John 6:63, John 6:68, John 8:47, John 15:7, Romans 10:8, Romans 10:17, Ephesians 5:26, Ephesians 6:17) Using the *rhema* word means that we have specific words that are individually tailored for each unique situation we face. In our spiritual warfare, we arm ourselves with the specific Word of God for the individual confrontations we meet and we have an invincible weapon that ensures us unquestionable victory.

Until David took the city of Jerusalem, it had never been captured. When Joshua came into the Promised Land, he defeated the king of Jerusalem, but the city itself was never taken. (Joshua 10:23-24, 15:63) The Jebusites boasted that Jerusalem was so secure that its guards were the blind and the lame men. (II Samuel 5:6) Its natural position made it virtually invincible; therefore, it was unnecessary to position the able-bodied soldiers there. These strong warriors were used elsewhere while the rejects defended the city. The city actually defended itself since it was built on the top of high cliffs with deep ravines surrounding it. When an attack would come, all these handicapped soldiers had to do was to simply push boulders over the edge of the cliff upon the approaching forces -- they did not need to be marksmen or skilled warriors.

David outfoxed the Jebusites by sending some men up the water duct to take the city from the inside. After David took the city, Jerusalem then became his stronghold. From the city of Jerusalem, we learn a lesson concerning strongholds: their power is in their natural position; you don't have to have a strong warrior inside a stronghold to be able to protect it because the stronghold itself is its own protection. The devil doesn't have to be strong. If he is able to fill our minds and hearts with lame ideas and blind assumptions, he can easily defend the strongholds of our lives.

A number of years ago, a contestant in a beauty contest knew that she was going to lose to one of the other entries, so she decided to resort to dubious means to defeat her. Her tactic to get the girl out of the completion was to curse her by telling her that every time she looked in the mirror, she would see how ugly she was. The curse worked, and the front-runner dropped out of the completion. In fact, she totally dropped out of life and spent the rest of her life as a recluse in her house. She spent all of her fortune on beauty products and cosmetic surgeries. No matter how many people tried to convince her that she was still a gorgeous lady, she never overcame the lie that had was planted in her mind during that pageant. It was a lame idea, but it took root in the stronghold of her mind and destroyer her future and life.

One of the unique characteristics of strongholds is that

they are positioned so that in the event of an attack, enemies would actually bring destruction upon themselves. In Sri Lanka, I have climbed to the top of Sigiriya, the spectacular "Lion Rock" fortress on top a gigantic rock whose sheer walls rise about twelve hundred feet above its luscious green jungle surroundings. This fortress, built in AD 473, was surrounded by huge slaps of stone that were triggered with rope mechanisms so that an avalanche of destruction would instantly engulf any intruding army. In Israel, I was able to climb the equally impressive fortress of Masada that was built by King Herod. This encampment poised atop the thirteen-hundred-foot precipice became the last bastion of the Jewish people against the Roman invasion. When the legion laid siege to the fortress in AD 72, the Romans realized that the only way to take the stronghold was to build a circumvallation wall to allow them to approach the plateau. They forced Jewish slaves to haul in the thousands of tons of stones and earth that it took to build the ramp because the attackers knew that the Jews in the fortress would not kill their national brethren. Otherwise, the Jews hold-up in the fortress would have pummeled their attackers to death with their arsenal of rocks. From my vantage point perched atop Sigiriya or Masada, thinking of the sheer insanity of launching an attack against either of these strongholds, I began to gain a perspective of how well defensible our position is Christ can and should be if we only renew our minds to become strongholds of truth rather than citadels for the enemy's blind assumptions and lame ideas.

Becoming a Prayer Warrior

Prayer is the battle for which we get dressed in Ephesians 6:11-17; yet how many messages do we hear about the getting dressed and how few do we hear about the actual battle? The old rhyme tells us that it's "one for the money, two for the show, three to get ready, and four to go." Let's not get all dressed up with nowhere to go! Paul tells us that we must enter into "all prayer," meaning all types of prayer. Prayer is an all-encompassing factor in the Christian life. We are directed to pray all the time (I Thessalonians 5:17), in every place (I Timothy 2:8), with every kind of prayer (Ephesians 6:18), about everything (Philippians 4:6), for all people (I Timothy 2:1). The biblical summation on the topic is found in James 5:16, "The effectual fervent prayer of a righteous man availeth much."

The Apostle Paul admonished us to pray always with all prayer in Ephesians 6:18. Literally translated from the Greek, his command to us was to pray with all kinds of prayer and to do this on a regular and ongoing basis. There are many components to prayer and many types of praying. One of the many kinds of prayer mentioned in the scriptures is confession -- a cleansing of our souls and a elimination of the obstacles between ourselves and God though acknowledging our sins which include both our wrongdoings and our shortcomings. (Psalm 51:1) Another kind of prayer is thanksgiving -- a prayer of appreciation (Psalm 107:1) and faith in that we can actually speak forth thanksgiving as we are still making requests for prayers that have not yet been answered (Philippians 4:6). As we thank God for what He has already done and thank Him for what He has promised to do, we have no reason to worry whether our requests will be granted. Another kind of prayer is praise and worship -- focusing on what God does and who He is. When we concentrate on Jehovah Rapha (the Lord our Healer), it is easy to receive healing. When we acknowledge Jehovah Jirah (the Lord our Provider), it is easy to receive the supply for all our needs. When we focus on Jehovah Shalom (the Lord our Peace), it is easy to have peace in the face of any storm. When we focus on Jehovah Nissi (the Lord our Victory Banner), it is easy to go into any conflict knowing that we will come out victoriously. When we focus on Jehovah Shammah (the Lord Who is There), it is easy to know that He is our ever-present help in time of trouble or difficulty. Another form of prayer is meditation -- contemplation on the person of God as well as His works and His words. (Psalms 1:2, 63:6, 77:12) Another form of prayer is called supplication or petition. This is an earnest and sincere entreaty of God. (Philippians 4:6, Hebrews 5:7) Although this type of prayer speaks of a humble request, it does not imply begging. Because of our relationship to God as adopted sons, we can boldly make our petitions before the throne of God our Father. Closely akin to this kind of prayer is intercession -- a petitioning on behalf of others. This prayer is when we care for the requests of others with the same -- or even a greater -- level of intensity as we would exhibit when praying for our own needs. This is what Abraham did for the wicked cities of Sodom and Gomorrah in Genesis 18:23-32 and what Moses did for the rebellious Israelites in Exodus 32:30-32. Sometimes this kind of praying leads into travailing -- an agonizing prayer of warfare that breaks through demonic as well as our human resistance to God's perfect will. (Luke 22:44, Galatians 4:19, I Thessalonians 2:9) Persistent prayer is a prayer that doesn't give up. (Hebrews 6:12) Persistent prayer may be repeated prayer. Elijah had to pray seven times before he saw the cloud that was only the size of a man's hand. But it is effective prayer. When the cloud did come, it brought a flood that inundated the whole vicinity. (I Kings 18:42-44)

Paul goes on to say that our prayers must be in the spirit. Although most translations capitalize the word to indicate that Paul was referring to the Holy Spirit, it is just as accurate to use a small "s" since both are possible from the Greek text. If the small "s" is used, the meaning of the passage would be that the prayer has to come from our human spirit rather than from our soulical nature -- the mind, the will, the emotion. Of course, the only way to get beyond our soulical motivation is to be directed by the Holy Spirit; therefore, the same message is communicated whether we use the capitalized "S" or the small "s." Before we go any further with the discussion of prayer in the spirit, let's back up a few words and notice that Paul referred to the offensive weapon in our armament as the sword of the spirit. Again, we could have the same discussion as to whether to capitalize the "S" or leave it small, but we could come to the same conclusion. The Word of God is only powerful when the Holy Spirit quickens it to our human spirits. (John 6:63, II Corinthians 3:6) Since that life-giving quickening comes through our human spirits, we again see that the Word of God only becomes a formidable weapon when its use comes from our human spirits under the anointing of the Holy Spirit. In the final analysis, our real power in spiritual warfare is prayers laced with the truths and principles of the Word of God that come from our human spirits under the direction and anointing of the Holy Spirit.

This dimension is opened to us when we allow the Holy Spirit to work through our spirits and assist us in our communication to God. (Romans 8:26-27) Most often this kind of praying is associated with prayer in unknown tongues, but the Holy Spirit can also anoint and direct prayers in our native language. (I Corinthians 14:15) Prayer in the spiritual realm is prayer that builds us up on our faith (Jude 20), that brings results for others (Ephesians 6:18), and that is in accordance with the Father's will and mind (I Corinthians 2:11). When we pray under the Holy Spirit's direction and know that our prayers are in alignment with the Lord's *rhema* will, we can have confidence that He will answer our prayers (I John 5:14-15) and that everything will work out for our best interest (Romans 8:28).

Prayer is our offensive weapon that changes things that we could never influence through brute force, military action, or litigation. Dick Eastman, a world-renowned teacher on prayer, shares a couple testimonies that prove this truth. On an expedition into Bhutan, he and his team were impressed with the controlling grip that Buddhism has on the country. As they prayed while walking around one of the main temples, one of the young men in their party said something to the effect of, "Lord, let fire out of heaven come down and consume this place." Within just hours, an electrical storm came up and lightning struck the main Buddhist temple in the country -- not the one where they were praying, but actually one that was of even more significance. The centuries-old wooden structure was totally consumed within minutes. But that's not the end of the story; not only was the physical temple destroyed, but the spiritual stronghold of Buddhism began to crumble. Within a few years, a secular government replaced the strict Buddhist regime that had dominated the country and kept it isolated from the rest of the world for hundreds of years. Before long, reports of a move of the Lord and the birth of a thriving Christian fellowship began to surface in this once forbidden land. Another story relates to a legal battle that was being waged over a television station in the United States. Dick and a group of students from his school of prayer had met for an all-day prayer session at a Christian television station. The president of the Christian network came in early in the day and said that he had planned to join them; however, he had to meet with attorneys that day concerning an issue with another station in the area that was broadcasting pornographic programming. As the group prayed that day, they occasionally remembered the issue. To their surprise, the president of the network showed up to join them before the day had ended. When they asked him how the meeting was going, he responded that the whole thing had been dropped because a very strong wind had suddenly come out of perfectly clear weather and had blown down the broadcast tower of the ungodly company. They had gone out of business without the attorneys having to challenge their broadcast permits!

Knowing Our Enemy

Paul said that he didn't shadow box or box against the wind. (I Corinthians 9:26) We know the story of the little boy named Peter who cried "Wolf!" and all the men of the town would come out prepared to fight the wolf. After he cried "Wolf!" so many times, the men no longer heeded his cry. When the wolf really did come, Peter and his sheep were all damaged or killed because there was a real wolf. There is a real enemy we have to fight against, and we do have to prepare ourselves to fight.

The first thing we need to recognize is that there is a devil called Satan. Most of the time, we don't actually fight against the devil himself. He is the commander and chief, and we are fighting against his soldiers, who are called demons.

Occasionally, we need to fight against natural forces in the world when these natural forces are under demonic control. The classic example of the authority of the Spirit exercised through a believer would be when Pat Robertson saw a hurricane coming in from the ocean headed right toward his Christian television station in Virginia Beach. Standing on the sands of the Atlantic Coast, he pointed his finger toward the ocean and commanded the hurricane to be turned back. The hurricane immediately turned eastward into the ocean instead of coming to the land!

Many times we have to fight against disease. Disease may be a natural force but it may be under demonic control. God has placed everything in the universe for a purpose. After He created the universe, He said, "It is good." (Genesis 1:25) He created bacteria and called them good. It was only after the devil got hold of the bacteria that they became dangerous, malignant, and detrimental to our lives. Disease is a destructive force of an enemy's power against us, and we have to do spiritual warfare against it.

There are some people who are under demonic control. Sometimes we have to literally fight against such a person. When a person is working under demonic control, that person has to be stopped. Sometimes those persons are in political situations. As long as these leaders are willingly receptive to demon influence, these evil spirits inside them will continue to work through these human leaders. In this case, we have to physically fight against these men. Although we know that we don't wrestle against flesh and blood, if these individuals desire that demonic power inside themselves, we must not only resist the spirit but also wage spiritual warfare toward that individual. Adolph Hitler would be one example of a person who was under demonic influence. There had to be spiritual warfare as well as physical warfare zeroed in on him, not just against a nebulous demon force.

Another area where we need to fight the enemy is in our thought realm. One of the major keys to being an overcoming Christian is the renewing of the mind. We are new creatures with a totally new mind set from what we had before. In II Corinthians 10:4-5, Paul tells us that we have to bring every thought into captivity and make every thought obedient to Christ. There are many thoughts that try to exalt themselves against the knowledge of Christ; such thoughts have to be removed. In John 8:44, Jesus tells us that the devil is a liar and the father of all lies. We have to recognize when he is speaking, know what thoughts he is giving us, realize that they are lies, and remove them.

I guess you would have to say that I'm a bit sassy, but sometimes I find that being a bit "over the edge" helps get the point across. When I was working as a prayer counselor at the altar after Sunday morning service, a lady came up with a need. "All week, the devil's been telling me that I have cancer." I nodded and said, "So, what's your prayer request." She then repeated the same statement, "All week, the devil's been telling me that I have cancer." Again I nodded politely and repeated my question, "So, what's your prayer request." Again she repeated the same statement, and again I posed the same question. This volley went on for a couple more rounds until she became observably agitated. Finally, I interrupted the routine with, "You don't have a problem with cancer; you have a problem with listening to the devil." (As harassing as I might have been, at least, I didn't tell her what I was tempted to say, "You don't have a problem with cancer; you have a problem with stupidity.") I then reminded her from John 8:44 that the devil is a liar and that there is no truth in him. I surmised that since the devil was telling her that she had cancer, the only logical scriptural conclusion would be that she doesn't! Wow! How liberating to understand that the only real power the devil has is to deceive us into believing that he actually has power to harm us!

Picking Our Battleground

Warfare assumes that there is a battleground. There is a place where the two opposing forces lock in on one another. For every war, there is a battlefield on which it must be fought. In I Thessalonians 2:18, Paul says to us, "Wherefore we would have come unto you, even I Paul, once and again; but Satan hindered us." There was a battleground that Paul had to go through before he was able to get to Thessalonica. There is an arena for our struggles against Satan. Either he calls it, or we call it. In the story of Joshua as he went into the Promised Land, he was the one who chose where the battle was to be arrayed. He was always careful except in one situation. In the battle of Ai (Joshua chapters seven and eight), he went out to fight at the city itself, and he wound up having to flee. The next time, he chose the battlefield at God's direction. Pretending to flee, he ran away from the city, drawing their army into the open plain away from the city where his ambushing forces attacked. When he chose the battlefield, he won triumphantly. In sports, there is a "home court advantage." On our home court, we have first-hand experience of trying to score a point from any given spot -- having scored from that spot in practice, we feel confident that we can also score in the real game. When we play on our home court, we also have the advantage of knowing that our fans are going to be in the stands rooting us on.

We have to know that somebody is going to call where this battle is going to be fought, and it is better for us to be the determinants instead of letting the devil draw us to his territory. Choose the place in your life where you wish to draw the line in the sand; don't wait until the devil gets the advantage and then try to fight him on his battlefield.

There is one thing that we need to see about Paul. At his trial in Caesarea, his accusers came from Jerusalem to try to have him extradited back to the city to be tried, but Paul refused to go back to Jerusalem. He had a divine mandate to go to Rome, and he knew that if he went back to

Jerusalem, he would be ambushed on the way or die in Jerusalem. Choosing his battlefield, he appealed to Caesar. (Acts 25:9-12) In II Corinthians 11:23-28, Paul gives us a list of the things that had come against him. He was on the battlefield when he was on a ship. He was on the battlefield when he was traveling. He was on the battlefield when he was thrown into prison. He was confronted every step of the way -- whether it was on the ship or in prison or whether he was among his churchmen, countrymen, or aliens -- but he always knew how to push the battle into an arena where he knew he had an advantage. Every one of these battlefields occurred when he was attacking the devil's kingdom, not when he was defending himself against the aggressions of the enemy. He kept the devil so busy defending himself that Satan never had a chance to choose the battlefield. He had to meet Paul where he was on his assault into the devil's territory. There is a battlefield, and we have to be the ones to decide where the battle lines are going to be drawn. We must pick an arena where we can fight aggressively, not defensively. We must do the same for our families, our ministries, our careers -- everything that is valuable to us.

Many times battle lines are drawn in our finances, and we have to determine that we are in control of the battlefield. I would prefer that my battle in finances be in how much I'm giving away rather than having enough to meet my needs. Some people are always struggling with paying their bills and keeping their set lifestyle. But we can draw the battlefield away from the area of getting enough to make the mortgage into the area of giving. If by faith we can pledge a gift to the work of God or desire to raise our giving above the simple tithe, the battle is on the grounds of giving rather than receiving. We know how to draw the devil out of his field and onto our court.

Many times the battle is drawn in the area of our health. We have to draw the devil out of the area of sickness and disease and simply standing for our health. It is always more of an adventure for the battle to be in the area of believing God to heal others, rather than fighting the devil to keep ourselves from dying. If we start to feel sick, we should find someone who is sick and pray for him. If we take that aggressive step of moving out of having our own needs met to blessing others, it draws the attack out of the enemy's battlefield and into another battlefield where we are on the offensive rather than the defensive.

Sometimes our spiritual growth, prayer life, and Bible reading time become the battlefield. When we determine that we are going to read the Bible, the devil determines that we are going to fall asleep. We could read the entire newspaper from cover to cover and not doze off, but if we sit down and read the Bible we start getting drowsy. That's because the devil has drawn us into battle. We have to push beyond that. The devil wants to call us into battle over the area of our spiritual growth and our prayer life. But we must resist him and push ourselves beyond that.

Many times the battlefield is drawn in the area of our family. Sometime the devil will want our sanity to be the battleground. Sometimes the arena of battle may be relationship to our joy, our peace, or our living beyond worry and anxiousness. Our vision and our direction may be a realm of the battlefield. Sometimes our mission, organization, and discipline are areas of our battlefield. Quite often, morals are the areas of a battlefield. Sometimes accidents and death are areas of a battlefield. We have to push forward beyond those things into strength and into positions where we don't fight on the devil's battlefield, but he fights on ours.

Notice that in the parable Jesus gave about spiritual warfare concerning a strong man who was keeping his house when the stronger one came, bound him, and plundered his goods that it was the stronger one (the believer) who chose the attack grounds. "No man can enter into a strong man's house, and spoil his goods, except he will first bind the strong man; and then he will spoil his house." (Mark 3:27) We should be in the area of determining where the battlefield is going to be. Instead of spending all our time in spiritual warfare trying to get all of our needs met, we can do spiritual warfare on the offensive and begin taking things away from the devil. We can take souls away from the devil -- plunder hell and populate heaven. We can push beyond the battlefields where he would like to engage us and put him on the defensive in trying to protect his own territory. We move the frontline beyond our territory and push it into his. If we can keep him engaged with our offenses, then our defense has taken care of itself. If we have been fighting offensively as well as defensively, then he doesn't have any ability to get into our realm and steal from us.

Choosing Our Weapons

Warfare assumes weapons. We don't go out to fight unless we have weapons. As Christians, we have a number of weapons and we need to learn to use them. In the Living Bible, Ken Taylor translates II Corinthians 6:7 as, "All of the godly man's arsenal -- weapons of defense, and weapons of attack -- have been ours." Let's take a look at what is actually included in this arsenal of spiritual weapons.

First, he listed purity, the ability to keep a right heart attitude in the midst of conflict. The Old Testament character Joseph could serve as an excellent example. (Genesis 37:2-36, 39:1-50:25) Even though he went through the pit, slavery, and prison, he always kept the attitude that God meant for everything to come out for good in his life. He went through hell with a heavenly attitude.

Next, Paul mentioned knowledge, knowing -- not hoping or wishing -- that God is on our side. Notice in each of the following scriptures from three different writers that each author tells us that his key is that he knows something:

> My brethren, count it all joy when ye fall into divers temptations; Knowing this, that the trying of your faith worketh patience. But let patience have her perfect work, that ye may be perfect and entire, wanting nothing. (James 1:2-4)
> For ye had compassion of me in my bonds, and took joyfully the spoiling of your goods, knowing in yourselves that ye have in heaven a better and an enduring substance. (Hebrews 10:34)
> And not only so, but we glory in tribulations also: knowing that tribulation worketh patience; And patience, experience; and experience, hope: And hope maketh not ashamed; because the love of God is shed abroad in our hearts by the Holy Ghost which is given unto us. (Romans 5:3-5)

Paul's third entry is longsuffering, the determination to never give up. The prize is given only to the one who finishes the course. The promise of salvation is relegated to those who endure to the end. We must be like Joshua and Caleb who, even though they had to put up with forty years in the desert because of other people's unbelief, kept their faith and eventually entered and possessed the Promised Land. (Numbers 13:1-14:38) Winston Churchill once addressed a class of graduating college seniors at their commencement by gruffly charging them, "Never give up!" He took a deep breath and bellowed out a second time, "Never give up!" Then after his third demand that they never give up, he took his seat. Dr. Lester Sumrall will forever live in the hearts of future generations as the man who would not quit. His testimonial tape entitled "I Did Not Quit" has inspired and challenged countless ministers and laymen to keep at the task God has given them.

Kindness, helping even our enemies, is Paul's fourth item of weaponry. The Philippian jailer had beaten Paul and left him bound and bleeding while creepy, crawly things slithered across his back. Since his hands were tied, he could not defend himself from their invasion and infection. Yet, when the jailer was ready to commit suicide, Paul rushed to his rescue and saved his life -- and then his soul. (Acts 16:22-34) Jesus taught us, "Love your enemies, bless them that curse you, do good to them that hate you, and pray for them which despitefully use you, and persecute you." (Matthew 5:44)

Paul calls his next entry simply the Holy Ghost. I'm certain that he meant to imply the entire influence of the Spirit in a Christian's life -- the gifts of the Spirit, the fruit of the Spirit (I Corinthians 12:8-10), living in the Spirit (Galatians 5:25), walking in the Spirit (Galatians 5:16), being spiritually minded (Romans 8:6), and being led by Spirit so as to not fulfill the lusts of the flesh (Galatians 5:18).

Love unfeigned -- or as the New King James Version

says "sincere love" -- might seem to be a strange implement for warfare, but it appears prominently as the next entry on Paul's list. In the New Testament time, most upper class families displayed marble statues in their homes and yards. If these marble statues were chipped or cracked they were often patched with wax. In the statuary shops, the flawless items were marked as being sincere (without wax). Paul's weapon -- and ours -- is flawless and genuine love, with no façade, which prepares us to become overcomers in our times of struggle.

> Whosoever believeth that Jesus is the Christ is born of God: and every one that loveth him that begat loveth him also that is begotten of him. By this we know that we love the children of God, when we love God, and keep his commandments. For this is the love of God, that we keep his commandments: and his commandments are not grievous. For whatsoever is born of God overcometh the world: and this is the victory that overcometh the world, even our faith. (I John 5:1-4)

Jesus really raised the bar on the idea of love unfeigned when He told us that we were to love our enemies. (Matthew 5:44; Luke 6:27, 35) This kind of behavior is so against the human nature that if it doesn't draw our enemies to the Christ inside us, it will drive them crazy trying to figure out what's happening. Seriously, history is full of testimonies of Christians who -- even when facing martyrdom -- used this weapon of unfeigned love on their executioners and won them to Christ. Many of the stories have follow-up chapters of the faith of those who came to Christ through the love of those whom they were persecuting. Many even wound up joining them on the chopping block or at the fiery stake to give their own lives for the Lord.

The word of truth appears next. Here Paul contrasted

Satan's strongholds of deception that he mentioned in chapter ten verses three through five against the positive mind of God that he talked about in chapter four verses sixteen through eighteen. Satan's thoughts are actually lies that make us slaves; God's thoughts are truths that set us free. Paul had determined to focus on the liberating thoughts of God's truth. Paul's focus was on the streets of gold, not the stones hitting him in the head; the loving embrace of Jesus, not the strong arm of the Roman beating him; his eternal home, not the present tribulation. He was so focused on the heaven he was going to that he barely noticed the hell he was going through.

When Paul added the power of God to his armament belt, I believe that he was talking about God's constructive -- not destructive -- power. Even though he was writing about warfare, I doubt that he was like James and John -- the Sons of Thunder -- who wanted to call down heavenly fire upon their opponents when Jesus replied that they did not know what spirit they were of. (Luke 9:54-55) I believe that he was praying exactly as the first church did when they encountered their initial persecution. In Acts 4:29-30, when the church prayed after the first confrontation, they did not ask God to "get" their enemies! Rather, they asked God to continue to stretch forth His hand and heal through them.

When Paul adds the armor of righteousness, it is apparent that this phrase is a summarizing statement because he uses a different Greek preposition to introduce it. All the above attitudes and actions must be abounding (on our right hand and on our left hand) in order for us to have victory. One translation says that these weapons serve as both our offense and our defense.

Because the apostle employed each of these weapons on a continual basis, he could say in verse four of chapter ten that the weapons of his warfare were not carnal but mighty through God to the pulling down of strongholds and in chapter two, verse fourteen that God always caused him to triumph.

And the Winner is...

When it looked like there was no possible way out, one of the soldiers lamented, "It looks like we should surrender without a fight." His companion rejoined, "I recognize those words, but the order you put them in makes no sense."

When there is a war, there is always someone who wins. Jesus is the victor. He has the keys of death and hell. (Revelation 1:18) He bruised the head of the serpent and of the seed of the serpent. (Genesis 3:15) Ephesians 2:6 and Colossians 3:1 tell us that we too are victors because we are seated in heavenly places with Christ far above the principalities, powers, and spiritual forces. When we enter spiritual warfare, one of the major assumptions is that warfare means that there is a winner -- and it might as well be me. In fact it will be me! "Now thanks be unto God, which always causeth us to triumph in Christ, and maketh manifest the savour of his knowledge by us in every place." (II Corinthians 2:14) Just as the Romans celebrated their victories with grandiose victory marches through the Arch d' Triumph, our lives are expected to be one continual gala parade of victorious testimonies!

But we are not just victors -- we are more than conquerors. (Romans 8:37) When asked what it means to be more than a conqueror, one Bible teacher explained it with the analogy of a prizefighter and his wife. The boxer went into the ring with a vicious antagonist. After suffering blows, lacerations, contusions, and bruises, he finally landed the winning punch that sent his opponent to the mat. He then crawled out of the ring as the champion -- a conqueror -- and was handed a sizable check for having won the bout. As soon as he arrived home, his wife happily took the check and started spending it. She did not have to go into the ring and take any blows or lose any blood, but she got the cash -- she was more than a conqueror. In the spirit realm, we are just like that wife; we get all the rewards even though it was Christ who faced the enemy and defeated him at the cross. We do not have to do the battling -- in fact, we couldn't even if it were up to us to do so. We must learn, as did Jehosaphat, to stand still and see the salvation of the Lord. (II Chronicles 20:17) No matter how much we think that we might be able to accomplish with our travailing intercession, languishing fasts, or vehement spiritual warring, we must be cautious not to go back to "conqueror mentality" when we can have "more than conqueror mentality."

Be strong, put on the full armor, and then stand!

What the Devil?

Witches, warlocks, haunted houses, ghosts, poltergeists, extraterrestrials, multiple personalities, imaginary friends, voices in our heads, things that go bump in the night, the monsters under our kids' beds, premonitions, messages and even visits from beyond the grave. What are they? Where do they come from? Are they even real? Yes, they are real, and I've had my fair share of encounters to prove it.

It was a dark and stormy night -- well, actually it wasn't stormy, and it wasn't any darker than any other ordinary night. But the events of that evening seem to fit so perfectly into one of those "dark and stormy night" stories that I just couldn't resist the intro line. In fact, the evening began as a rather ordinary one. I was visiting the University of North Carolina's Wilmington campus. Since it was only a few miles from Wrightsville Beach, our group had decided to stay with a friend who managed an old beachfront hotel on the Atlantic Coast. The old building had long since seen its better days and was soon to be bulldozed down to make way for the parking lot for a modern condominium. After checking into our rooms, we headed back to town for a Bible study on campus. About halfway through the study, a young lady sort of floated into the room. With an out-of-this-world daze in her eye, she looked around and asked, "What is this place?" We responded that it was a Bible study and that she was welcome to sit down and join us. Her reply was that she was just walking down the hall when "the spirit" told her to come in, so she took a seat and glared around the room as we completed our session. After the meeting, several of the students talked and prayed with her until it was time to leave the room. At that point, one of the students who was traveling with me suggested that our guest come back to the hotel with us for some further counseling.

She decided to accept the invitation, and we headed for the beach. As soon as we parked and headed toward the building, I began to feel the uncanny sensation that I was walking into a horror movie. The eeriness continued to mount as we entered the back door. Inside, the kitchen was vibrant with an unearthly presence. On the table we found a large box with a note attached. It was from a young man who had just received Jesus into his heart that day. It explained that, with his new life, he wanted to totally break from the old one that had involved a lot of occultism. The box contained all his occult books that he wished to destroy but was afraid to do by himself. His request was that we burn them for him. Eager to rid the house of the unholy manifestation, we grabbed the box and headed for the fireplace. In that it was winter and that this relic of a hotel was anything but airtight, a roaring fire was already waiting for us in the lobby. All the lobby furniture was huddled around the fireplace as a resort for all the guests as we tried to defend ourselves against the chilly ocean breezes that blew almost as freely through the hotel as they did on the windswept sand dunes outside. Our group, including the new guest, grabbed seats close to the open fireplace as we began to toss the occult books into the flames.

Our new friend, in an almost hypnotic voice, began to talk about each of the books as she pulled them out of the box, "This is an expensive book; we can't burn it. This is a nice one, why do you want to destroy it?" We all knew that something was wrong, but no one knew what to do or say. Upon our insistence, every book made it to the inferno, but the evil presence remained. It was at that point that we realized that the demon was not in the books but in the co-ed from the campus -- so we began to try to cast it out. Notice that I said "try." None of us had ever done that before, so we were novices using the trial-and-error method. At one point, we asked the young lady if she wanted Jesus to come into her heart so that she could go to heaven; the response was, "Oh, heaven will be boring -- just sitting around playing a harp." At that instant, I realized that I had not been talking to the young lady at all, but that my conversation was with a demon that was speaking through her. I demanded that the spirit be quiet so that the girl could hear and respond. Calling her name, I commanded her to answer me and to receive Jesus into her heart and join me in commanding the demon to leave. She did -- and she was free. No longer did she stare with hollow eyes into space. No longer did she speak in a monotone. No longer did she move catatonically. Suddenly she was a vibrant, vivacious young girl. But, she had one major problem -- she didn't know where she was or how she had gotten there. Looking at her watch, she exclaimed, "How did it get this late? I've only been gone about ten minutes!" In actuality, she had been in the hotel lobby at least two hours plus all the time she was in the classroom on campus. The spirit that had been controlling her had actually obliterated all reality out of her consciousness and she had been living in the twilight zone under its domination. That night she was free at last, and she continued to live a free and productive life in Christ.

Since that day, I have met many others under the devil's control and have seen them set free in the name of Jesus. When I rebuked the spirit in one man who came to my office for prayer, the demon threw him across the room, and he crashed into the wall. When he picked himself up, he began to hop around the room like a frog as his mouth began to spew out the vilest forms of blasphemy and profanity. Yet, at the name of Jesus, he was instantly free and stood to his feet a new man. When he came back for follow-up counseling the next day, he stopped at the receptionist's desk and asked to see me. The receptionist called me to inform me that a gentleman claiming to be the one who had been in the prior day was there for an appointment. She added, "But this isn't the same man; I've never seen this man before." He was so radically changed that it showed on his face.

Another young man came to me for counseling and prayer. Under terrible bondage of low self-esteem, he refused to look up. Recognizing this as a demonic torment, I put my hand under his chin and forced him to raise his head and look me straight in the eyes. After ministering deliverance to him, I took him with me to a Christian fellowship meeting. Before long, people who had known the lad for several months began to come up and welcome the newcomer to the group. They had never seen him with his head up and did not recognize him as the same person they had known for a number of weeks.

As I faced these various demonic encounters, I have learned some valuable lessons about the awesome destructive power of the devil and the magnificent restoration power of Jesus. It could be summed up in the little motto, "The devil is a bad devil, but God is a good God." It's the same message as conveyed in John 10:10, "The thief cometh not, but for to steal, and to kill, and to destroy: I am come that they might have life, and that they might have it more abundantly."

Possibly the most important lesson I've learned in dealing with these alien forces is that the subjects have to want to be free in order to have victory over the spirits that are tormenting them. I've dealt with individuals who have pulled their hair, ripped their clothes off, burned themselves with cigarettes, and even cut themselves while under the demonic control; however, not a one of them has ever been able to touch me during the confrontation. Why? Because I know that I don't have to be subject to these spirits. They respect my authority over them. They can only torment those who allow them to. One young lady was miraculously delivered of a number of very powerful spirits yet still was addicted to smoking cigarettes. That seemingly insignificant fault had an unbreakable hold over her. As I prayed for her, a man's voice spoke through her lips, "I'm not coming out because she wants me here." Upon questioning the young lady, I found that she was actually a willing victim of the nicotine spirit. It did not come out until she decided that she really wanted it out.

There is an old story that made the rounds a number of years ago about a man who had come for prayer at an evangelistic campaign. As the evangelist was going down the line laying hands on the people who were there to receive ministry, he eventually came to the man in question.

When the minister started to pray for the gentleman, he discerned that a demonic spirit possessed the man and he proceeded to cast it out, "Come out, you spirit of lust!" As if a scene from a V-8 commercial, the man jerked the evangelist's hand from his forehead and slapped his own hand in its place screaming, "Stay in! Stay in!" Well, I guess this story to be a joke, but there is a lot of truth behind it. Some people simply don't want to be free from the demonic influences in their lives. And if an individual doesn't want to be free, it is very unlikely that anyone can make much difference by praying for him. I remember one Indian lady who came to my wife for deliverance. Even after she had spent several sessions ministering to the woman, nothing positive had happened. Finally, I stepped in on one of the sessions and asked if the woman really wanted to be free; when she could not answer positively, I advised my wife to let her alone because she was only creating her own problems. Jesus told a story that is recorded in Matthew chapter twelve and Luke chapter eleven in which He explained that the end result if a spirit is cast out of a person and that person allows it to come back is that the individual's final situation will be much worse than his initial condition. I feared that this is what would happen to the woman if we were able to cast out the spirit but she really didn't care about being free -- it would come back to tempt her and she would allow it to come back in, worsening her condition. My wife and I have seen this sort of willing acceptance of demonic torment in a number of cases, especially when sexual pleasures are associated with the demonic influence.

One other area I have noticed that causes people to willingly retain demonic control over their lives can be identified in the cases where the spirit's influence brings attention to the person under its power. One woman came to our church asking for special prayer but noted that she had already been to all the "big" evangelists and they couldn't do anything for her. Of course, we did everything we could to help her; but, of course, she left in just as bad a shape as when she came because she really wasn't wanting help -- just another "notch on her pistol handle" that she could use as proof when she bragged about how bad her case was. I remember one woman in Nepal who had really become the center of attention as she rolled on the floor from one side of the room to the other. She was actually rolling back and forth between a couple groups of ladies who were trying to minister to her. Eventually, my wife noticed what was happening and realized that the woman was only trying to make a big show to get the attention of everyone in the room, taking the focus off of Jesus and putting it on her. At that point, my wife stopped her and asked if she really wanted to be free or just wanted everyone to see her. When the lady realized that Peggy understood what was happening, she admitted her desire for attention and asked to be set free -- and she was gloriously delivered!

One of the trophies that I keep in my bookcase is a large hunting knife that was presented to me by a young man in desperation. A spirit of murder had controlled him, tormenting him with the thought of killing his sister and dismembering her body. After the demonic control over his life was broken, he went home as a man finally at peace with himself. Yet that night, he awoke with the haunting nightmare that he was going through with the diabolic plan. It was only after he returned to my office the next morning and surrendered this weapon to me that he knew that he was free from the spirit of murder. Any physical property that has been dedicated to the devil's purposes, (such as that knife) or any item of pagan worship or witchcraft (such as the occult books in the hotel) can become lodging places for demonic entities that can remain to torment those susceptible to their control.

I was cleaning a large attic room of a house that we had just purchased. The building was empty and I was alone as I swept away years of dust. Suddenly, I felt an evil presence as I worked my way across the middle of the hardwood floor. Clutching the broom a little tighter, I looked around to locate the source of this unwelcome invader. My attention was drawn upward to the light fixture directly above my head. I noticed immediately that there was a sort of secret cubbyhole above the light where a horizontal platform for mounting the fixture had been suspended from the slanted ceiling. After locating a chair, I climbed up to investigate that mysterious secret compartment. Inside, I found the most horrible cache of pornographic literature imaginable. After removing the literature, the demonic presence left the room. Later, a group of us prayed over the house and asked that God anoint the building so that people would be aware of the Holy Spirit's presence when they came in. We wanted to totally replace the evil with good. We knew that our prayer had taken effect on the day a man came knocking at the front door to ask what kind of house it was. He claimed to have felt the presence of Jesus as he walked down the sidewalk in front of the home. Territory that had been given over to Satan was now reclaimed for Jesus.

A bright young high school student contacted me for advice and counseling on his new life in Christ. As we corresponded over a period of several months, he suggested that he and his father would be happy for me to visit when I was in the area. It turned out that I was scheduled to visit a college campus not far from their home, so I arranged to drive down a day early and spend the night with them. I had no idea what awaited me as I walked in the front door. There were several strange items that caught my eye. For example: a lady's dress was hanging on a coat rack in the entrance -- even though the father and the mother were divorced and she had not lived in the home for many years. When the father showed me to my room he explained that everything inside had been brought intact from a Mississippi River boat that had served as a floating house of prostitution in the 1800s. I was to sleep in a reconstructed brothel.

It was only after dinner and after my young friend retired for the night that I found out that the father was the head of the local gay rights movement. He was one of the few who had come out of the closet in the 1970s. It was a very uneasy conversation, but we spent some time discussing what the Bible says about homosexuality and that Jesus was willing to release him if he wanted to be free. A crocodile tear and a weak confession later, he asked for me to lay hands on him for deliverance. I soon discovered that all he wanted was for me to get close enough for him to lay his hands on me! The instant that he reached out for me, I screamed out, "In the name of Jesus!" and he was hurled backwards across the room. At that point, I left him sprawled across the furniture and retired to my room. It was the most restless night of my life. All night long, there was the sound of clawing on the walls and door. I knew that demon spirits were trying to attack me, but I was convinced of one fact more concretely: I was under the shadow of the Almighty, and those things would not be able to penetrate God's protective wing. (Psalm 91:1-4) The next morning, I left for my college meeting, realizing the difference between that house and my own. In each, there was demonic manifestation. In one, it was not tolerated and it had to leave; in the other, it was welcomed and it had taken total control.

One interesting postscript to that story is that when I arrived for my college meeting, I found that my host had left his apartment door open for me even though he was in class at the time I was expected to arrive. So, I went in and made myself at home. While resting on his sofa, I drifted off into a sound sleep from the exhaustion of the night's spiritual warfare. Suddenly, I was jolted to reality as the radio came on and began to blare an evangelist's fifteen-minute show into my ear. When the man finished his quarter hour of edification and exhortation, the radio shut itself off and I drifted back to sleep. Later my host arrived and I recounted the events of the past twenty-four hours. I ended the story by describing how neat it was that he had the radio set to turn on and off for the program and that the message was a blessing to me after the challenging encounter. With eyes like saucers, my host explained that he had not set the radio and, in fact, that it wasn't even programmable!

On another occasion, I was invited to attend a church service to hear one of my students minister. As a special guest, I was also called to the front to help minister to the people during the altar service. Two young girls approached me for prayer to receive the baptism in the Holy Spirit. As I ministered to them, I could hear a commotion across the church. It soon became obvious that a demonic manifestation was out of control at the other end of the altar. Finally, the girls began to speak in other tongues, and I turned them over to one of the elders for further instruction. When the elder looked at the girls and warned them that a man was having demons cast out of him and that they should keep praying or the demons might go into them, I knew that the church was ignorant of the spiritual world. After reassuring the girls that they could not arbitrarily be taken over by unclean spirits, I went over to assist in the deliverance. I found the man sprawled out on the floor covered with open Bibles and even the big brass cross from the front of the church. They were trying every gimmick possible to make that spirit go out of the man. At least they were not beating him on the head as I have seen done in Nepal. IN fact, there has been at least one case in Nepal where a parishioner actually died form a beating that his pastor inflicted upon him while trying to drive a demon out of him. However, the biblical way is that the name of Jesus be used in faith. When I did that, he was instantly set free. The lesson here is that God's work done God's way produces God's results.

On another occasion, a guest minister at our church had "set some ground rules" concerning ministry during his crusade; no one other than his personal staff was to minister or lay hands on anyone during the services. Even though I was an associate minister at the church, I was submitted to that authority and was, therefore, carefully avoiding any form of intervention in situations that arose during his campaign. However, when a woman began to manifest demonic control as she lay on the floor flipping back and forth, I was really disturbed that such a blatant display was going on unchecked. I simply spoke the name of Jesus and exerted my authority under my breath without ever leaving my seat. As soon as I whispered the command for her to stop, she suddenly became calm and restful.

There definitely is a malevolent supernatural world, and it does invade our lives -- more often than we would be willing to deal with. Unfortunately, most of us are unprepared for those confrontations and do not know how to handle them when they occur. Like the congregation who threw Bibles and even the brass cross on the chest of the possessed man, we try all sorts of gimmicks rather than knowing how to apply truly biblical principles and take proper action. A priest and four nuns in Romania were jailed over an attempted exorcism in which the subject died. This was sort of the reverse of the popular movie, <u>The Exorcist</u> in which the priest who tried to set the girl free wound up losing his life. Of course, we can surmise that that was only a scene play -- until we overhear one of the leading exorcists in the Catholic Church confess that a little part of him dies every time he performs an exorcism. But not all deliverance blunders are fatal; some are just plain silly. For instance, a popular teaching based on Jesus' example in Mark 5:9 and Luke 8:30 held that the minister should always ask the demon's name before trying to cast it out of a tormented subject. I see two major flaws in this approach: first, because the devil is a liar (John 8:44) there would be no real reason to believe his answer; and, secondly, if the spirit has never had the authority to speak through the subject's voice, we are actually acting counterproductively by giving it more authority when we are in the process of trying to break its power. In connection with this practice, I once witnessed an over-zealous young minister attack what he thought to be a spirit in a timid little twelve-year-old girl with the command, "What is your name?" When the horrified youngster responded, "Suzie," I figured that it was time to pull the exorcist off and try to speak prophetically into the little girl's life with edification, exhortation, and comfort. (I Corinthians 14:3) One so-called exorcist who had catalogued all the evil spirits and given them numbers was ministering to an acquaintance of mine when he supposedly discerned that she was harboring two demons. At that point, he proceeded to cast out "demon number sixteen" and "demon number seventy-three." The poor lady went to her grave without ever knowing what these two wicked entities that were supposedly cast out of her were. Of course, I do remember that in one of this gentleman's books one of the demons he had cataloged was post-nasal drip. It's at that point that I want to put a new spin on the interpretation of Luke 11:14, "And he was casting out a devil, and it was dumb." Instead of the "dumb" meaning "mute," I would question if the more contemporary meaning might be applicable. And instead of applying the term to the spirit, I would rather think that it was more appropriate to attribute it to the one trying to cast it out.

The fact that the devil is a liar who doesn't even recognize that his lies are not even intelligent enough to benefit his cause was demonstrated when we were ministering to a woman in Nepal and a man's voice with typical broken English spoke out of her lips, "Me too done." We obviously knew that he wasn't gone if he was still manifesting that way through the lady! On another occasion, I witnessed a young Nepali girl fall to the floor under what everyone thought to be the Holy Spirit anointing. However, I discerned that it was only the devil trying to hide. Thinking that no one would notice his camouflage, he felt safe while hiding inside the defenseless girl -- that is until I came to her and demanded that she be set free. Instantly, the spirit tried to manifest by throwing the girl's body violently about on the floor. Of course, we commanded it to stop and come out. As soon as we called upon the name of Jesus, she became normal again.

Another fad that swept through Christian circles several

years ago was the practice of spitting up demons. In fact, many so-called deliverance ministers actually carried a supply of plastic bags and paper towels with them so that they were always ready to catch these "demons" when they came out. I suppose the first time I encountered this sort of thing was when my wife and I were just acquaintances, before we even started dating. Her roommate came home from a meeting where one of these ministers had supposedly cast a demon out of her and had actually put it in a paper bag for her to take home with her. When Peggy called me to ask whether it was safe to have that sort of thing in her apartment, it was all I could do to restrain myself from laughing. If it were a spirit, how could it possibly be kept captive in a paper bag? Apparently the "exorcist" was basing his theology on the story of the genie in Aladdin's lamp in A Thousand and One Arabian Nights rather than the lessons of Jesus in the Bible!

One major problem I have observed around the world is that most people actually don't recognize demonic manifestations when they occur. In the Dominican Republic, I witnessed an unusual manifestation in one of the church leaders. Not being totally familiar with the local customs, I was not exactly sure what her role in the church was; however, I had no doubt that she was a significant leader in the congregation since she had a special seat of honor in the front of the church. During the praise and worship time, she began to dance around -- nothing unusual at this point since all of us, including myself, were celebrating with dancing. However, her motions became more and more animated until they could actually be called violent jerks. Several members of the congregation stepped up and grabbed hands, forming a human chain encircling her. Apparently, they were accustomed to having her act this way and had developed a system to protect her from crashing against the furnishings as she pulsated about. All the while, I was becoming more and more uneasy with the way she was thrashing about and I felt more and more certain that an evil spirit was manifesting through her. However, as a stranger in the church, I felt that it was out of place for me to intervene -- especially since this was one of their leaders and it seemed to be an accepted practice for her to act like this. Eventually she collapsed to the floor, and I could not stay in the pew any longer. Dropping to my knees beside her, I grabbed the lady and began to rebuke the spirit in English. A bloodcurdling cry exploded from her lips, and she sat up free from the power that had controlled her. When the missionary came over to interpret, she thanked me for recognizing the spirit and breaking its power. She went on to say that it had tormented her for a number of months and that it had come upon her when she had visited a voodoo-infected area bordering Haiti, the nation that shares their island.

A second problem I have noticed in this arena is that even when people do recognize the existence of demonic forces, they don't know how to deal with them. I remember seeing a television documentary of an exorcism that took some sixteen hours before the ministers saw any relief for the girl they were praying for. It happened that this particular incident occurred in a Catholic setting and was filled with sprinkling holy water, calling upon the names of saints, and many other rituals. However, the girl was visibly changed by the end of the almost-day-long session. As I scrutinized what was happening in the documentary, I noticed that it was only after the exorcist actually used the name of Jesus that the girl received her deliverance. I couldn't help but wonder why he didn't try that hours earlier. Before anyone assumes that I am taking a punch at the Catholic church, let me hasten to remind you that all the other stories I've shared -- including the one about the brass cross -- happened in Protestant settings. In fact, some Protestants have a tendency to invent rituals that make the splashing of holy water seem almost mundane -- things like shouting in tongues, jerking and thrashing their hands, and even renting airplanes so they can fly into the high places to do spiritual warfare in the very places where, according to Ephesians 6:12, the spiritual forces reside.

Probably the most significant problem is a false evaluation of the power and authority of the demonic realm on the one hand and of the believer on the other hand. I remember making the last round through the church one night after a very long day during a convention. It was now almost eleven o'clock and I had been there since before sun-up and would be back again before dawn the next day as well. However, I couldn't leave and lock the building until everyone was out. My problem was one elder who was frantically trying to cast a demon out of a man. When I walked up to the scene, I overheard the elder shout, "We'll stay here till 2 AM if that's what it takes to get you out!" At that point, I realized two things: first, that he certainly was not going to be with me at daybreak the next morning; and secondly, that he didn't understand spiritual authority. I promptly interrupted his deliverance session with a little teaching session by explaining that he had relinquished all authority he might have had prior to that time by setting a limit of two o'clock. I explained that the spirit recognized that the elder had attributed a certain amount of authority to it and, therefore, it had settled in with no thought of budging right up through one fifty-nine.

A good portion of the remainder of this book will focus on the specific issue of understanding exactly what authority we have and what powers the demonic forces can exert. But before we leave this section, I'd like to add just one more observation about the abilities demonstrated by these evil powers: they are not limited in terms of language. I have had many experiences in some of the most far-flung corners of the globe -- places like Nepal, Sri Lanka, and Haiti -- where I could command in English and the demon spirits would respond immediately. Even though the person to whom I was ministering could not understand English, the spirit inside the person would know exactly what I was saying when I would demand that it be silent or that it look at me. I've even had conversations with individuals who could speak back to me in perfect English while under demonic control -- yet they could speak only the local language once they were set free. This truth will prove to be significant when we realize that the real authority we have in demonic encounters is through the spoken word!

Where Did the Devil Come From?

Before we get into the discussion about how we are to confront these alien demonic forces, perhaps it is appropriate to understand where they came from and where they are going. With this knowledge, we get a bit better perspective of where we stand in the overall scheme of things when we enter into conflict with them. The Bible gives us two accounts of the origin of the devil.

> How art thou fallen from heaven, O Lucifer, son of the morning! how art thou cut down to the ground, which didst weaken the nations! For thou hast said in thine heart, I will ascend into heaven, I will exalt my throne above the stars of God: I will sit also upon the mount of the congregation, in the sides of the north: I will ascend above the heights of the clouds; I will be like the most High. Yet thou shalt be brought down to hell, to the sides of the pit. They that see thee shall narrowly look upon thee, and consider thee, saying, Is this the man that made the earth to tremble, that did shake kingdoms; That made the world as a wilderness, and destroyed the cities thereof; that opened not the house of his prisoners? (Isaiah 14:12-17)
>
> Son of man, take up a lamentation upon the king of Tyrus, and say unto him, Thus saith the Lord GOD; Thou sealest up the sum, full of wisdom, and perfect in beauty. Thou hast been in Eden the garden of God; every precious stone was thy covering, the sardius, topaz, and the diamond, the beryl, the onyx, and the jasper, the sapphire, the emerald, and the carbuncle, and gold: the workmanship of thy tabrets and of thy pipes was prepared in thee in the day that thou

wast created. Thou art the anointed cherub that covereth; and I have set thee so: thou wast upon the holy mountain of God; thou hast walked up and down in the midst of the stones of fire. Thou wast perfect in thy ways from the day that thou wast created, till iniquity was found in thee. By the multitude of thy merchandise they have filled the midst of thee with violence, and thou hast sinned: therefore I will cast thee as profane out of the mountain of God: and I will destroy thee, O covering cherub, from the midst of the stones of fire. Thine heart was lifted up because of thy beauty, thou hast corrupted thy wisdom by reason of thy brightness: I will cast thee to the ground, I will lay thee before kings, that they may behold thee.   Thou hast defiled thy sanctuaries by the multitude of thine iniquities, by the iniquity of thy traffick; therefore will I bring forth a fire from the midst of thee, it shall devour thee, and I will bring thee to ashes upon the earth in the sight of all them that behold thee. All they that know thee among the people shall be astonished at thee: thou shalt be a terror, and never shalt thou be any more. (Ezekiel 28:12-19)

From these passages, we see the depiction of a magnificently beautiful creature who was overtaken with pride and tried to exalt himself to be equal with God. We learn that his original name was Lucifer, that he was originally a cherub -- or angel -- in heaven. His attempt to exalt himself resulted in not only his own personal downfall but also the destruction of cities and nations as he was cast down to the earth. Jesus adds that He personally witnessed Satan's fall as if it were lightning out of heaven down to the earth (Luke 10:18) and that he and his demonic assistants are doomed to an eventual judgment in hell (Matthew 25:41). We also learn from the life of Jesus that the demonic spirits recognize that they have only a set period of time before they are to be brought into judgment. (Matthew 8:29) The book of Revelation rounds out the picture of this diabolical creature by depicting his original fall and his final demise.

> And there appeared another wonder in heaven; and behold a great red dragon, having seven heads and ten horns, and seven crowns upon his heads. And his tail drew the third part of the stars of heaven, and did cast them to the earth: and the dragon stood before the woman which was ready to be delivered, for to devour her child as soon as it was born…And there was war in heaven: Michael and his angels fought against the dragon; and the dragon fought and his angels, And prevailed not; neither was their place found any more in heaven. And the great dragon was cast out, that old serpent, called the Devil, and Satan, which deceiveth the whole world: he was cast out into the earth, and his angels were cast out with him. And I heard a loud voice saying in heaven, Now is come salvation, and strength, and the kingdom of our God, and the power of his Christ: for the accuser of our brethren is cast down, which accused them before our God day and night. And I heard a loud voice saying in heaven, Now is come salvation, and strength, and the kingdom of our God, and the power of his Christ: for the accuser of our brethren is cast down, which accused them before our God day and night. And

they overcame him by the blood of the Lamb, and by the word of their testimony; and they loved not their lives unto the death. Therefore rejoice, ye heavens, and ye that dwell in them. Woe to the inhabiters of the earth and of the sea! for the devil is come down unto you, having great wrath, because he knoweth that he hath but a short time. (verses 12:3-4, 7-12)

And cast him into the bottomless pit, and shut him up, and set a seal upon him, that he should deceive the nations no more, till the thousand years should be fulfilled: and after that he must be loosed a little season...And when the thousand years are expired, Satan shall be loosed out of his prison...And the devil that deceived them was cast into the lake of fire and brimstone, where the beast and the false prophet are, and shall be tormented day and night for ever and ever. (verses 20:3, 7, 10)

From these verses, we learn a number of significant points including that he dragged down one third of the angels with him when he fell. Revelation 1:20 plainly states that stars in this vision are to be understood as angels; therefore, by using scripture to interpret scripture, we can see that Lucifer not only doomed himself through his rebellion but also destroyed one out every three of the angels in heaven. As tragic as that may be, we must remember that this means that there are still twice as many good angles as there are evil ones. Just as these evil angels try to torment us, the good ones are constantly ready to minister to and bless us. (Matthew 4:11; Hebrews 1:7; Psalm 34:7, 91:11-12) Additionally, we see that there is coming a time when Satan will be bound for a thousand years and then loosed for a short season only to meet his ultimate judgment of eternal torment in the lake of fire.

Before we move on, let's make a bit of a detour and make a short study of the cosmos of our universe. In II Corinthians 12:2, Paul wrote of a man who was caught up to the third heaven, which happens to be the heaven were God lives and rules from His throne room. If there is a third heaven, there must obviously be a first and second one as well. But what are they? Well, it is easy to see that the first heaven is the atmosphere around us -- the heavens through which the birds, planes, and Superman fly. (Pardon me; I just couldn't stop myself.) But the identity of the second heaven can be an enigma wrapped up in a puzzle unless we have a bit of spiritual insight. In order to begin to unwrap this mystery, let's take a quick journey back to the days of Elisha the prophet. At one point in his ministry, the Syrian army surrounded him and intended to capture him. When the prophet's servant peeked out the door, he discovered the massive troop encampment and reported the dire situation to his master. Elisha replied that there was nothing to fear since there were more on their side than in the enemy's army. The servant replied that he wasn't exactly the brightest student in his math class but that he could count well enough to see that there were only two of them and hundreds of the others. Finally, Elisha prayed and asked the Lord to open his servant's eyes so that he could see that the mountain was full of horses and chariots of fire. (II Kings 6:17) Apparently, what the servant saw was the angelic host that the Lord had sent to encamp around the prophet as his protection. But it is also obvious that these angelic hosts operated in the same time-space continuum as the physical world although they were usually not visible. What happened that day was that God supernaturally removed the dimension wall that separates the first heaven (the physical atmosphere in which we live) and the second heaven (the spiritual world were demons and angels dwell). When we remember that Satan is called "the prince of the power of the air" (Ephesians 2:2), we can readily surmise that he must have a spiritual system of power organized in the atmosphere of our planet even though we are not able to see him and his forces. Adding to this understanding that there are at least four references in scripture to the fact that spiritual dominion is exerted in heavenly places (Ephesians 1:3, 20; 2:6; 3:10), it becomes apparent that the second heaven occupies the same space as does the first heaven yet is distinguished from the first heaven in that it is of a spiritual nature rather than a physical one.

Going back to the passages in Revelation, I would like to suggest that we can see a three-stage progression in the devil's demise. First, he was kicked out of the third heaven in verses three and four. This is the same event discussed in Isaiah, Ezekiel, and in Jesus' reference to his lightning-like fall. In this expulsion from the third heaven, he fell to the earth and took his place of authority in the second heaven. In verses seven through twelve, we see a second conflict in which he is cast out of the second heaven. Though many Bible teachers would claim this to be a continuation of the original conflict, careful observation of the details of the story would place this struggle at a much later date. First of all, he is described as the one who deceives the whole world, something he was not able to do before his original fall in that the humans had not yet populated the world and his first act of deception occurred in the Garden of Eden after his expulsion from the third heaven. He is also called the one who accuses the brethren, again, a charge that could only be levied against him after the Garden of Eden experience. Another significant fact is that a voice from heaven announced that salvation, the strength and the kingdom of God, and the power of Christ had come -- a proclamation that was totally out of place at the time of the fall of Satan from the third heaven. Rather than being a time of salvation and celebration, it was actually the beginning of the period of conflict and torment for the human race. Additionally, we must note that the scriptures state that the devil recognized that his time is short -- another contradiction of facts if this passage is speaking of the original fall of Lucifer. Instead, this passage seems to make reference to the end of his time as the devil rather than his initiation as Satan. Taking all these factors into consideration, it seems likely that the verses are referring to an event which has not yet come to pass -- a time when Satan and his demonic associates will be cast out of the second heaven. When this happens, they will no longer have the advantage of invisibility and will be exposed for who they are -- an astonishing confirmation of the words of both Isaiah and Ezekiel. "They that see thee shall narrowly look upon thee, and consider thee, saying, Is this the man that made the earth to tremble, that did shake kingdoms; That made the world as a wilderness, and destroyed the cities thereof; that opened not the house of his prisoners?" (Isaiah 14:16-17) "I will bring thee to ashes upon the earth in the sight of all them that behold thee. All they that know thee among the people shall be astonished at thee: thou shalt be a terror, and never shalt thou be any more." (Ezekiel 28:18-19) His sojourn in the first heaven will apparently be very short as it gives way to his final expulsion out of all three heavens to the hell of the lake of fire.

One interesting question could be raised in regards to the coming judgment of Satan and his angels. According to II Peter 2:4 and Jude 6, at least part -- if not all -- the fallen angels are already cast down to hell and are delivered in chains as they await their final judgment. If this is the case, then why are they still a threat to us? The answer to this question will become sufficiently clear as we continue our study into the nature of Satan's authority in this present world, but for now, let it suffice to answer that even though these demonic forces are bound there is no mention that they are also gagged. In other words, their opportunity for physical harassment may be abated but their ability to speak and inundate the world with their lies has not yet been squelched. (Revelation 12:15) To comprehend the power that words can have even when the speaker is physically restrained, just think of the effect of Paul's epistles that he wrote while occupying a long series of jail cells across the Roman Empire or the impact of <u>Pilgrim's Progress</u> that has been translated into more than two hundred languages and has never been out of print since John Bunyan penned the allegory in England's Bedfordshire County Jail in 1678. The power of these chained spirits has little to do with how strong or numerous they are but what they are able to say and cause us to believe.

Now that we have a bit of the background of where the devil and his demonic hoard came from and a glimpse into the future as to where they are going, it is time for us to explore what it means to live in a world in which these invisible forces are able to exert very real influence. Though most of our encounters with these forces will not be as dramatic as some of the ones illustrated in the previous section of this book, they are just as real and must be dealt with just as authoritatively. Even though it is not very often that we encounter women speaking with men's voices -- on a daily basis, we do encounter people whose words are just as directly influenced by the enemy. Even though we may never have to deal with men leaping around the room acting like frogs -- on a daily basis, we must deal with individuals who are degraded to the sub-human level of some animal instinct through the work of the destroyer. The horror of the story is that it is all too often that we find these individuals even within ourselves. In all these encounters, we need to know exactly where we fit into God's overall scheme of putting the devil in his place.

Power, Might, and Dominion

In Ephesians chapter six, the Apostle Paul gives us what is possibly the most authoritative instruction concerning confronting these supernatural forces. To understand who and what these spiritual authorities are, let's look at the Greek words that Paul uses. It is also important to understand the words he uses to describe what we have on our side as well. There are several different Greek words that appear in Ephesians showing us that Christian power is different from that of the enemy. When we come out to fight the enemy, both the Christian and the enemy have power -- but not only do the two forces have power on different levels, their powers are actually in different categories.

It is amazing to me how many people have assumed that God and the devil are equals and that spiritual warfare is a toss-up. The truth is that in our spiritual struggle our team has a different kind of power from that of the other team. To understand this concept, we must look at the Greek words that are used to speak of the kinds of power and authority that God has given to us as believers and the kind of authority that the devil and his forces have in their possession.

Ephesians 1:19-20 speaks of the surpassing greatness of His power toward us who believe in accordance with the working of the strength of His might. On God's side, there is power, strength, and might. He is seated in a position of authority far above all forces of the devil which are listed in Ephesians 1:21 as principality, power, might, dominion, and every name that is named. The word translated "greatness" is *megethos*, from the Greek word *megas*, meaning "big." This term, meaning "the great power of God," appears only this one time in all the New Testament and refers to power on a grand scale. I find it fascinating that Paul also amplifies this already super powerful term by preceding it with the word "exceeding" which also means "on a grand scale, more than enough." Thus, he emphasized that God's power is on a grand scale that is even grander than grand!

"Power" here is the Greek word *dunamis*, which is sometimes translated as "might." It denotes "inherent ability, capability, ability to perform anything" -- the power to carry something into effect, or power in action. Some other passages where we find the term *dunamis* include Matthew 6:13, "Thine is the kingdom and the power" and numerous verses referring to the mighty acts of Jesus' ministry, such as healing the sick and casting out devils. (Luke 4:36, 5:17) In Philippians 3:10, it is used in reference to the resurrection of Jesus from the dead. This term also speaks to us about the enduements of the Holy Spirit in the lives of believers. (Luke 9:1) Power, or *dunamis*, means "God's ability to do powerful, mighty acts, the miracle working power of God, God's strength." The Discovery Bible defines *dunamis* as, "the inherent capability of someone or something to carry something out. It is the power by virtue of one's own ability and resources." One especially interesting reference is in Matthew 26:64 where it is used as a title or name for God Himself. There is one case where this term for power also refers to demonic forces: Matthew 24:29, "the powers of the heavens shall be shaken." In the book of Revelation, the word "power" appears in relationship to the working of God; however, in the one verse of Revelation 13:2 it refers to Satanic power, "the dragon gave him his power."

Basically, the word "power" is associated with the strength, might, and the demonstration of God. *Dunamis* is used when talking about casting out devils, healing the sick, the resurrection, and the moving of the Holy Spirit. In the entire New Testament the word *dunamis* is used many, many times to denote the working ability of the Lord. There are only a very few verses where *dunamis* is referred to as the devil's being able to exert power. The enemy does have some power and ability, but the overwhelming use of "power" in the New Testament is not on the devil's side; it is referring to God's power. When we are told to be strong in the Lord, the Greek word is *endunamo*, which means to have the *dunamis* (power, might) inside you.

The Greek word *iscus*, which speaks of actual strength, physical ability, and muscle movement, occurs only about a dozen times in the New Testament and is usually translated "strength," although it can also be translated as "might" and "power." The <u>Discovery</u> <u>Bible</u> defines this term as "the inherent strength, the strength as an endowment, strength residing in a person." It is used in Mark 12:30, 33 and Luke 10:27 where we are commanded to love God with all our strength. It is also found in Ephesians 6:10 which directs us to "be strong in the Lord and in the power of his might." In II Thessalonians 1:9, I Peter 4:11, II Peter 2:11, Revelation 5:12, 7:12, and 18:2 the term refers to the might of God. The New Testament never uses iscus in reference to the devil and his power; rather, it is always associated on the side of the Lord.

The Greek word translated in Ephesians 1:19 as "strength" is <u>k</u>ratos, which occurs twelve times in the New Testament and has a connotation of rulership. It consistently refers to the might and rule of God. In only one instance does it have a negative connotation -- Hebrews 2:14, where it talks about the strength of death. *Kratos* means force, strength, might, more especially pertaining to manifested power. Derived from the root *kra*, meaning "to correct or to complete," it also signifies dominion. <u>The</u> <u>Discovery</u> <u>Bible</u> defines it as "the manifested power, dominion, might, power that is exercised or applied and thence that which prevails, mastery or force."

According to Ephesians 1:19, we have ability in Christ that is in accordance with God's mighty dominion. This means that since God is in total dominion, the power that is within us is in direct proportion to that -- total and absolute. If we can get a grasp of the kind of dominion that God has and we understand that the exceeding greatness of the mighty ability that works through us is in direct proportion to God's unlimited power, we will come to a totally new revelation of the spiritual power we have. However, until we begin to believe how strong God is, we will never begin to recognize where we stand when we go into our spiritual warfare.

Ephesians 1:21 declares that Jesus is seated far above all principalities. This term referring to Satan's power is the Greek word *arkee* that means "principal one or beginning." It also means "the first rule." In most of the places where this word occurs in the New Testament, it is translated "beginning." The imagery conveyed through this term portrays a dynasty in the devil's kingdom with the prince or principality as the ruler or first one over a particular domain. According to Colossians 1:16, these principalities were first given their power and position by God; however, they fell from their positions because they aspired to something that was prohibited. The logical question to ask at this point would be, "If God created Lucifer and these now-fallen angels, and if their rulership and power was given to them by God -- did He give them equal authority with Himself?" The obvious answer is, "No." In fact, the scriptures directly answer this question for us by telling us that Lucifer sinned when he aspired to be equal with God. (Isaiah 14:13-14) Obviously, he and his fellow rebels were lower than God, or they would have not had a feeling that they needed to elevate themselves to become His equal. What this means for us today is that any satanic struggle that we may encounter is not going to be at our same level. The power that is working in our opponent is derived from the demonic forces that, even from creation, were inferior to the exceeding great power of God that is working in and through us!

In Romans 8:35 Paul asks, "Who shall separate us from the love of Christ?" He then goes on to answer his own question, "Nothing, not even principalities." (verse 38) These primary satanic forces cannot separate us from God's love. First Corinthians 15:24 assures us that we have put down all rule and all power over us. Ephesians 3:10 affirms that we believers have a point to prove to these demonic forces, "to the intent that now unto the principalities and powers in heavenly places might be known by the Church the manifold wisdom of God." Colossians 1:16, proclaims that Christ is the head over all principalities, and Colossians 2:15 adds that He has "spoiled" all these principalities -- literally meaning, as we have already learned, that He has stripped these demonic forces naked.

Ephesians 1:21 goes on to say that Christ is seated far above powers. The word for "power" that is used here is the Greek word *exousia* that means "the right to exercise power or authority." This term is the key word used for the devil's power, and it appears in most of the scriptures that refer to the power of the enemy. The Discovery Bible defines it as, "delegated power, authority, the power to act by virtue of the position that one holds. The right to act or use power."

Before we can delve into what is meant by the devil's power, we must first recognize that Christ, too, has this type of power. The term *exousia* appears in Matthew 7:29 that says that the people marveled at Jesus' teaching because he spoke as one having authority. The rabbis of Jesus' day had intellectual ability; they could argue and reason back and forth, but they had never cast out a devil. Not only did Jesus teach, but he also exercised authority over sickness and demons. In Matthew chapter eight, we find the story of a centurion who asked Jesus to simply speak the word so that his servant would be healed. Using the term *exousia* when he explained that he was a man under authority, the centurion indicated that he, therefore, understood the authority of Jesus' spoken words. The next chapter of Matthew contains the story of a palsy victim whom Jesus healed with the words, "But that ye may know that the Son of man hath power on earth to forgive sins, (then saith he to the sick of the palsy,) Arise, take up thy bed, and go unto thine house." In other words, Jesus was saying, "I have spoken a word of forgiveness. I could have spoken a word of healing. But I want you to know that I have authority in the earth to forgive sin." The authority He was demonstrating was His ability to speak supernaturally. It wasn't a matter of Jesus' doing a physical thing, such as a working of a miracle. Rather, it was a matter of speaking a word. There was a power (*exousia*) in His word to forgive sin and to heal the sick. Matthew 9:8 records the response to such a demonstration of *exousia*, "But when the multitudes saw it, they marvelled, and glorified God, which had given such power unto men."

It is in Matthew 10:1 that we find one of the most exciting verses on the topic of *exousia*. "And when he had called unto him his twelve disciples, he gave them power (*exousia*) against unclean spirits, to cast them out, and to heal all manner of sickness and all manner of disease." Jesus not only demonstrated to the people that He had *exousia* (power, authority), but He also gave that same authority to His disciples. When the disciples went out into the villages proclaiming the message that He had given to them, they were also able to heal the sick and cast out devils by *exousia* -- the words of their mouths. They did not have to grab the people and shake the demons or sicknesses out of them; they were empowered to bring about supernatural change by the power of their voices and the authority of their words. All too often, believers fail to understand what *exousia* is and how it works. On one of my early missions to Nepal when a Nepali lady started manifesting a demonic demonstration, all the other Christian women around her jumped on her and started pounding on her to beat the devil out. They didn't know about *exousia* until we taught them to speak to the demon with authority and make it come out.

After His death and resurrection, Jesus said to the disciples in Matthew 28:18-19, "All authority (*exousia*) is given to me in heaven and in earth. Go ye therefore...teach" and cause the people to observe what I command. When He told them to teach the people to observe all the things that He had commanded them, Jesus was again associating *exousia* with the spoken word. John 1:12 proclaims, "But as many as received him, to them gave he power (*exousia*) to become the sons of God, even to them that believe on his name." How does one become a son of God? According to Romans 10:10, it is with the heart that a man believes unto righteousness and with the mouth that confession is made unto salvation. With the heart we believe, but it is only when we confess it with the mouth that we receive salvation; the authority to become sons of God is released through the spoken word.

We read in Acts 26:12, "Whereupon as I went to Damascus with authority and commission from the chief priests." Saul was on his way to Damascus with words that had been given to him from the high priests in Jerusalem that he was in charge of arresting and persecuting the Christians. Saul did not carry weapons to execute his authority; he went to Damascus with a piece of paper giving him the *exousia* to arrest the Christians.

There is power in God's Word. The whole of heaven and earth were created by the spoken Word of God. (Genesis 1:3-25) Originally, the earth was without form and void; it was one big whirling pool of nothing. Then God looked into that chaos and said, "Light be!" and it was -- God created by the power of His word! He didn't mold and shape the moon with His hands; He just spoke, and it was created. He didn't use His might or force, all He had to do was use His authority. Jesus is the Word of God (John 1:1); He is not the thought of God but the physical manifestation of all the authority (*exousia*) of God. All that exists in God's vocal authority existed physically in Jesus. When we understand the power of the creative Word of God, we will realize that we don't have to put a lot of energy or muscle into bringing about supernatural changes; we just need to exercise the authority of the spoken word. This is exactly what the wise man Solomon meant when he wrote in Proverbs 18:21 that the very power of life and death is in the tongue.

Revelation chapter twenty tells us that when God decides to bind the devil up for a thousand years, He will not have to call myriads and myriads of angels to come fight the devil and pin him down long enough to throw him into prison. Verse one says, "And I saw an angel come down from heaven, having the key of the bottomless pit and a great chain in his hand." It only takes one angel. The devil doesn't have an overwhelming amount of strength, muscle, or energy. But his overwhelming ability is in being able to deceive men and bring them captive through his words. In fact, the devil only has power in those people who will listen to him. He will plant the seed in a very small way in the minds of his victims. He will keep drilling, drilling, and drilling until that thought gets inside of them. If they will listen to his thought, before long, they won't have the physical energy to stop doing what the devil is suggesting. His strength to work on his victims is really in the realm of his voice. Those who allow themselves to hear what he says will sooner or later come under his dominion.

The devil has been put under our feet. (Romans 16:20) We are seated far above him. (Ephesians 1:20-22, 2:6) We have been given the exceeding greatness of God's mighty power (*kratos* and *dunamis*). (Ephesians 1:19) Yet Satan still is characterized as having *exousia*. He can still speak those boastful and exalted words. We must guard our ears and guard our hearts so that his words don't get inside us. (Luke 8:18) We must understand that he is a liar and the father of lies (John 8:44) and that what he says are boastful words and vain imaginations (I Corinthians 10:5). If we understand that, we can then put his authority back down in the place it belongs, and we can exert the physical energy that we have over him. Two stories from the life of Jesus illustrate the fact that Satan's *exousia* is limited by God's permission for him to exert it.

In Luke 22:53 when the soldiers came to get Jesus in the garden before the crucifixion He said to them, "This is your hour and the power (*exousia*) of darkness." There was not an opportunity for the devil to do his work outside of God's timing. There was an appointed time when Satan was allowed to exercise his authority (*exousia*). Satan did not have full reign to do all he wanted to do. It was only in an appointed time that he was able to exert his authority. Too often, we give the devil too much credit. He doesn't have all power, might, or dominion. He is regulated and held back because God is in control. Throughout the gospel of John, Jesus spoke about His hour. (John 2:4; 7:30; 8:20; 12:23; 13:1; 16:21, 32) The citizens of Nazareth tried to push Him off a cliff, and at several points angry men took up stones to try to kill Him; but He continually pronounced, "My hour is not yet come." It was not until the Last Supper with His disciples that Jesus raised up His hands and said, "The hour is come." (John 17:1) At that point, there was a releasing of the authority of the devil to do what he had to do by putting evil thoughts into the hearts of men so that they could act on hell's desire to destroy Jesus.

John 19:10 relates another reference to *exousia*. Pilate said to Jesus, "Do you not know that I have the authority (*exousia*) to crucify you and the power to release you?" Jesus answered him and said, "You could have no power at all against me unless it has been given to you from above." Jesus' confrontation with Pontius Pilate was over this item for power. Pilate said that he had the authority (*exousia*) that by the words of his mouth he could either crucify or free Jesus. The thing that Pilate didn't understand was that it was God who gives men authority on earth. Pilate was given the authority.

The unfortunate -- even tragic -- truth is that we so-called believers often counter God's authority and allow Satan to exercise *exousia* in our lives. Yes, we are believers; unfortunately, we are believing the lies of the enemy. When the children of Israel came out of Egypt, Moses sent out twelve spies to look over the Promised Land. Two of the spies brought back a good report, but the other ten brought back a negative report. They reported,

"We were in our own sight as grasshoppers, and so we were in their sight." (Numbers 13:33) They listened to the lie of the devil. His *exousia* sapped the physical might and power from inside of them. They had the physical ability to take the land -- Caleb demonstrated it even forty-five years later when, as an eighty-five-year-old man, he took a mountain. When the children of Israel came under the power of Satan's *exousia*, it wiped out the *dunamis* and the *kratos* that they had. The flipside of the coin is revealed when Rahab told how the entire city of Jericho responded at the report that the Israelites were approaching, "And as soon as we had heard these things, our hearts did melt, neither did there remain any more courage in any man, because of you: for the LORD your God, he is God in heaven above, and in earth beneath." (Joshua 2:11) When they had heard the reports of how the God of Israel parted the Red Sea and drowned the Egyptian army, the *exousia* of the report overpowered them -- even though the events were some forty years prior. There was no more energy left in them to fight because they were bound up in fear of the Israelites. Here we have a paradoxical instance: the *exousia* of God had crippled the inhabitants of Canaan, whereas the Israelites never knew what certain victory awaited them because they had allowed themselves to be overtaken by the *exousia* of the enemy.

We can live either under the *exousia* of God, the strength that comes from hearing God's Word, or under the *exousia* that comes from hearing the devil's word. The devil's voice saps all the energy and power of God out of us. If we listen to God's voice, He can sap all the enemy's energy and make the demonic hoards weak before us.

Finally we can get back to our biblical passage -- I bet you thought I had forgotten! Ephesians chapter six goes on to say that we are seated far above "mights." The Greek word used here is *dunamis*. As we have already discovered, even though the devil does have *dunamis*, in the majority of cases when this word is found in the scripture it refers to the might of the Lord. Satan's might is never emphasized as is his authority.

Another quality attributed to Satan is dominion. This word (*kuriotas*) appears only four times in the New Testament (Ephesians 1:21, Colossians 1:16, II Peter 2:10, Jude 8). W. E. Vine writes of this term, "It denotes lordship, power or dominion, whether angelic or human. It indicates a degree in the angelic order in which it stands second." Generally, this term is used in relationship to Christians who are referred to as actually having the physical strength or might. The devil does have some physical might, but the word that generally describes what the devil has is *exousia* or authority.

Let's think back to what we have learned about how David took the city of Jerusalem. We learned that a stronghold's power is in its natural position; there doesn't have to be a strong warrior inside a stronghold to be able to protect it because the stronghold itself is its own protection. The devil doesn't have to be strong. If he is able to fill our minds and hearts with lame ideas and blind assumptions, he can easily defend the strongholds of our lives. Once he gets inside the stronghold, he can exercise *exousia*. He doesn't have to exercise *dunamis* or *kratos*. When the devil gets inside our thinking and begins to feed us with lies and deception, he saps whatever *dunamis* is inside us. On the other hand, the truth can get inside our strongholds and make them just as strong a fortification for the truth as they were for the devil's lies. The power of our mind is incredible. "For as he thinketh in his heart, so is he." (Proverbs 23:7) When we listen to the evil thoughts of defeat and we receive those thoughts, we are defeated. When the thoughts of God get into our minds and our spirits and fill us with thoughts of success, we are successful. One interesting side note is that when David took the city of Jerusalem, he armed it with his mighty men -- not the lame and blind men as did the Jebusites. In like fashion -- when Christ takes over our minds and hearts, He fortifies our strongholds with the powerful truths of the Word of God! (Philippians 4:7) We have already learned that we have weapons in our warfare that are not carnal but they are mighty in God and they pull down the strongholds where the enemy has set up camp. When we let the devil's *exousia* get a stronghold inside our lives, that *exousia* will destroy the *dunamis* and the *kratos* that God wants us to be able to exert. It will sap the physical ability out of us. We will faint before our enemy if we give his *exousia* a place in us.

If we submit ourselves to God and resist the devil as James 4:7 teaches us, the enemy has to flee. The Greek term used in this verse literally means to run away in terror just like a whipped dog will tuck its tail between its legs and escape danger. The devil doesn't tumble around on the floor trying to wrestle or fight with us, hoping that maybe he will win one or two rounds or at least get in a couple good blows or a lucky punch here and there. According to this biblical truth, he gets up and runs away. He may try to growl, but he cannot stand against us because we are walking in authority over him. But where does that authority come from? It comes from the weapons of our warfare that are more powerful than his lies -- the truths of the Word of God. Let's think back one more time to how David out-tricked the Jebusites when he took the city of Jerusalem from the lame and blind guards. According to II Samuel 5:8, the attack approach was through the water canal. In Ephesians 5:26, Paul uses water as a symbol of the Word of God. If this symbol can also be applied to the story of David's conquest of Jerusalem, we can see that the lesson exactly parallels biblical truth -- the only way we are to take control of the strongholds in our lives is to infiltrate them with the truth of the Word of God -- the weapon that is more powerful than the enemy's lies. One interesting footnote to this story is that the King James translation of this verse says that he sent his men into the city through the gutter. What a powerful thought -- what had been a gutter, filled with the garbage thoughts of this world, became the avenue through which the renewing and life-giving truths of God could invade!

Then Paul said that we do not wrestle against flesh and blood, but against principalities, powers, against spiritual hosts of wickedness in high places. The terms that are used are terms that have to do with magistrates or authorities. Just as our nation is divided into states, then counties, then cities, then precincts, the spiritual kingdom is set up in the same way. The first and foremost areas are principalities. As we have already learned, the word "principality" means "the first, the original." These spirits are the ruling spirits that control all the subsidiary spirits under them. In some cases, we may deal with a subsidiary spirit who rules over one specific thing; in other cases, we may deal with a principality spirit who has authority over many spirits in a large area. There are several examples of having confronted spirits that were principalities that rule over large areas.

A very prominent story comes from the life of Dr. Lester Sumrall, one of the great authorities on dealing with demonic power. When the Lord spoke to him to go to the Philippines to raise up a ministry there, He promised, "I will do more for you there than I have done for you anywhere else in your ministry." Knowing that there had never been any major Protestant revival in the Philippines in the history of the country and that there were very few Christians in the city, Bro. Sumrall went to Manila with great anticipation of what God was going to do. For the first several months, there was only a handful of people in his church. About the time that the congregation had grown to around fifty people, the Lord began impressing him that he was to build a barn to hold the coming harvest. So Bro. Sumrall started building a church that would seat twenty-five hundred people. He reasoned that he needed a building of at least that size since he had left a church in the US with over a thousand adults and a thousand children in the Sunday school each week, and the Lord had promised something bigger in the

Philippines. Everybody begged him not to build such a large a facility. His denomination thought that he would make them the laughing stock of the entire world -- building a church to seat over two thousand when he only had fifty members. Protestant missionaries and prominent church leaders came to Manila to stop him because they were afraid he would take their members to fill his church. But he refused to be swayed by their arguments because he knew that God would bring a revival such as the Philippines had never seen.

One night as he was getting ready for bed, he and his wife listened to the evening news. Suddenly bloodcurdling screaming and horrifying howls come across the airwaves. The news feature was the story of a young girl incarcerated in the Bilibid Prison in Manila who had been mysteriously bitten by unseen teeth. Medical doctors and prison wardens observed as tooth marks and blood mysteriously appeared on her body. From his missionary experience, Bro. Sumrall recognized that this was demonic power tormenting her, so he got out of bed and lay on the floor praying and travailing, asking God to send somebody to deliver her from the demon power. But the Lord answered him, "If you don't do it, it won't happen. You are the only one in this city who knows how to cast the devil out of her." At that point, Bro. Sumrall had no way of knowing that what would happen with this girl was the key that would open up his ministry in the Philippines.

He spent that night in prayer and fasting. The next morning, he called the contractor building the church. Since he was a personal friend of the mayor, the contractor got Bro. Sumrall into the mayor's office where Bro. Sumrall asked for permission to go into the prison to pray for the girl. The story of the girl had already hit the international news, and the city had sent out appeals for church leaders, psychiatrists, or somebody to come and help her -- but no one was able to deliver her. Bro. Sumrall went to pray for her, but he did not get a total victory the first day; so he went back again the second and third days. After three days of fasting and prayer he spoke to the spirit, and it left. Not only was the girl set free, but a remarkable thing happened in the city. Unbeknownst to Bro. Sumrall, the demon spirit in that young girl was the principality spirit that ruled the entire Philippines. And as soon as its power was broken, the entire spirit realm of the Philippines became defenseless against the attack of the gospel.

When Bro. Sumrall was ushered back into the mayor's office with the good news that the girl had been freed, the mayor was so pleased that he asked what Bro. Sumrall wanted in return. His request was for permission to have large open-air revival meetings every night on the main plaza of the city. Within a six-week period, one hundred fifty thousand people were converted to Christ. When construction of the church was complete and the dedication service was held, the church was so jammed packed that most of the crowd could not get inside. This is the kind of results that come when a principality that is ruling over a geographic area is broken.

There are different evil spirits that rule different areas of the country or the world. For instance, in Las Vegas there is a spirit of gambling and greed that rules over that city. I have watched people get off of an airplane and run to play the slot machines that were located between the arrival gate and the baggage claim before they even went to pick up their luggage. When a deadly fire struck the Las Vegas MGM Hotel, helicopters had to be brought in to help rescue the hundreds of guests who were trapped on the upper floors. In addition to the tragic loss of life, a more horrifying tragedy was that while the hotel was engulfed in a deadly inferno, the other casinos on the same block never lost a customer. The spirits of greed and gambling had gripped their victims so tightly that even though people were dying next door, the gamblers couldn't stop long enough to be concerned about them. They were possessed by the principality of the city.

Christians and Demons

When asked if a Christian could have a demon, one great Christian leader answered, "A Christian can have anything he has faith for!" Although his answer might seem to be a bit humorous, it really seems to "hit the nail on the head." The main problem we might have in understanding what he was saying is that most of us don't really realize what level of faith we have and what it is that we are using our faith to obtain. It doesn't matter how loudly we preach about healing, if we run to the doctor and the pharmacy as quickly as our unsaved neighbors do -- we don't have any more faith than they do. Regardless of how many Bible verses we may quote about prosperity, if we worry about money as much as our secular friends do -- we are at the same level of faith with them. The bottom line is that if we think and act like unsaved people (as Romans 12:2 said, are conformed to the world), we actually have the same kind of faith that the world has. If this is the case, we will get the same rewards for our faith that they get for theirs.

Although the Bible doesn't make distinction between possession, oppression, and other varying degrees of demonic activity, it does speak of those who were vexed (Luke 6:18, Acts 5:16), sore vexed (Matthew 17:15), and grievously vexed (Matthew 15:22) -- indicating that there are various intensities of demonic activity. However, all these cases use the same word in Greek, which could be literally translated as "demonized," meaning under the influence of a demon or demons.

As long as we inhabit planet earth, we are literally living in the devil's front yard. He is the god of this present world (II Corinthians 4:4), the prince and power of the air (Ephesians 2:2), and the prince of this world (John 15:11). Furthermore, we are in constant confrontation with the elaborate array of forces he has enforcing his power throughout his regime. (Ephesians 6:12) Therefore, as long as we share this planet with the devil and his hosts, we will experience some degree of demonization -- we will, to one degree or another, be under the influence of demons. Even the Apostle Paul acknowledged that the devil had a certain amount of control over his life. "Wherefore we would have come unto you, even I Paul, once and again; but Satan hindered us." (I Thessalonians 2:18) He wasn't in sin or rebellion; he wasn't sick or deranged; but he was controlled by the devil in that he could not do what he had determined to do. The force was external, but it still was a determining factor in his life. Because of the devil's influence, he could not do what he wanted to do and what was apparently the will of God for him. In the strictest sense of the term, he was demonized!

However, just because we live in the devil's territory does not mean that we live under his jurisdiction. We are given numerous admonitions that we do not live under his authority; on the contrary, he is under our authority:

> Behold, I give unto you power to tread on serpents and scorpions, and over all the power of the enemy: and nothing shall by any means hurt you. (Luke 10:19)
> Nay, in all these things we are more than conquerors through him that loved us." (Romans 8:37)
> I have written unto you, young men, because ye are strong, and the word of God abideth in you, and ye have overcome the wicked one. (I John 2:14)
> Ye are of God, little children, and have overcome them: because greater is he that is in you, than he that is in the world. (I John 4:4)
> And when he had called unto him his twelve disciples, he gave them power against unclean spirits, to cast them out, and to heal all manner of sickness and all manner of disease. (Matthew 10:1)

As we have already mentioned, the book of Job

provides us with a behind-the-scenes glimpse into the spiritual struggle that is going on over the lives of believers. Satan presented himself before God to do what he does best -- accuse the brethren. In this case, God taunted Satan by challenging him to examine the life of one of His servants that He knew would not waver no matter how severely he might be attacked. "And the LORD said unto Satan, Hast thou considered my servant Job, that there is none like him in the earth, a perfect and an upright man, one that feareth God, and escheweth evil?" (Job 1:8) Satan's response was that he had seen Job, but he couldn't touch him because there was a hedge around him. "Hast not thou made an hedge about him, and about his house, and about all that he hath on every side? thou hast blessed the work of his hands, and his substance is increased in the land." (Job 1:10) Even though the Lord permitted Satan to penetrate the hedge, he was not able to dissuade the righteous servant. Not so easily defeated, Satan pressed the Lord for permission to penetrate even further into Job's life. Even though he was permitted to attack Job in every way short of taking his physical life (Job 2:6), Satan still was not able to overcome God's trophy servant. The truth is that God is no respecter of persons (Acts 10:34); He doesn't put a hedge around one and leave the others unprotected. He has left us just as well protected as He did His servant Job with a shield of faith with which quenches all the fiery darts of the wicked one. (Ephesians 6:16)

The Christians at Galatia experienced a level of demonization which Paul called being "bewitched," literally meaning under the spell of a witch. "O foolish Galatians, who hath bewitched you, that ye should not obey the truth, before whose eyes Jesus Christ hath been evidently set forth, crucified among you?" (verse 3:1) The striking reality of this passage is that Paul addressed them as foolish and as not obeying the truth. The reason they came under such dramatic demonic control was because of their foolishness in not obeying the truth. Since these Christians had acted so unwisely and rebelliously, it is no wonder that the enemy attacked and overpowered them! Only when we, like the Galatians through foolishness and rebellion, put down that shield and invite the open attack of the enemy do we come under the debilitating influence of the devil.

Let's take a quick look at the lives of some biblical characters who through their foolishness and rebellion let down their shields and suffered severely. Samson was repeatedly tempted by Deliah to give her the secret of his strength. Each time he tried to trick her, he woke the next morning to find that she had attempted to take his strength by following the deceptive plan he had presented the evening before. It could be called the personification of foolishness when he finally told her the true secret to his superhuman power. Only the densest mind would not have figured that she was going to shave his head since she had already tried all the other methods he had presented to her. The end result was a spiritual demise that he did not expect. "And she said, The Philistines be upon thee, Samson. And he awoke out of his sleep, and said, I will go out as at other times before, and shake myself. And he wist not that the LORD was departed from him." (Judges 16:20) When King Saul had a similar spiritual calamity because of his rebellion and lack of wisdom, the scriptures are even more explicit that not only did he lose his connection with God but that the void left in his life was immediately filled by a harassing demonic spirit. "But the Spirit of the LORD departed from Saul, and an evil spirit from the LORD troubled him." (I Samuel 16:14) King David, Saul's successor to the throne, also came dangerously close to experiencing the Holy Spirit's departing from his life because of his rebellion against God and society through his adultery with Bathsheba and the murderous plot he executed against her husband. The prayer he prayed for restoration after these heinous sins reveals how close he had come to slipping over the edge. "Cast me not away from thy presence; and take not thy holy spirit from me. Restore unto me the joy of thy salvation; and uphold me with thy free spirit." (Psalms 51:11-12)

In trying to bring the church of Galatia into correction, Paul instructed them how to live wisely and avoid further rebellion by simply saying that they should stand firm in their liberty and to walk in the Spirit.

> Stand fast therefore in the liberty wherewith Christ hath made us free, and be not entangled again with the yoke of bondage. (verse 5:1)
>
> This I say then, Walk in the Spirit, and ye shall not fulfil the lust of the flesh. For the flesh lusteth against the Spirit, and the Spirit against the flesh: and these are contrary the one to the other: so that ye cannot do the things that ye would. But if ye be led of the Spirit, ye are not under the law. Now the works of the flesh are manifest, which are these; Adultery, fornication, uncleanness, lasciviousness, Idolatry, witchcraft, hatred, variance, emulations, wrath, strife, seditions, heresies, Envyings, murders, drunkenness, revellings, and such like: of the which I tell you before, as I have also told you in time past, that they which do such things shall not inherit the kingdom of God. (verses 5:16-21)

Many of these sins, although called works of the flesh, are specifically identified in the scripture as being associated with demonic spirits. Adultery, fornication, and lasciviousness would be associated with the spirit of whoredoms we learn about in Hosea 4:12 and 5:4. Unclean spirits are the most frequently mentioned demons in the New Testament. Witchcraft and idolatry are constantly associated with pagan spirits throughout the Old Testament. Emulations is the same as the spirit jealousy discussed in

Numbers 5:14 and 30. Heresies are certainly the doctrines of devils that Paul mentioned in I Timothy 4:1. Though drunkenness is never specifically listed as a spirit, it is set in deliberate contrast to the influence of the Holy Spirit in Ephesians 5:18 suggesting its spiritual nature.

It is interesting that the apostle did not insist that they needed a deliverance session in which a demon spirit would be cast out; he simply said that they needed to get out of the flesh and into the spirit. In a sort of the-best-defense-is-a-good-offense approach, Paul advocated that there was great deliverance and freedom available to them by taking positive action. When writing to the Romans, he advised them that the process by which they would escape from their worldly level and advance to the divine nature was to renew their minds. "Be not conformed to this world: but be ye transformed by the renewing of your mind, that ye may prove what is that good, and acceptable, and perfect, will of God." (Romans 12: 2)

Paul had already learned this lesson in his own life when, harassed by a tormenting spirit, he cried out to the Lord for deliverance and was answered that he did not need external divine intervention. In fact, the authority he needed to combat and overcome his demonic foe was already inside him.

> And lest I should be exalted above measure through the abundance of the revelations, there was given to me a thorn in the flesh, the messenger of Satan to buffet me, lest I should be exalted above measure. For this thing I besought the Lord thrice, that it might depart from me. And he said unto me, My grace is sufficient for thee: for my strength is made perfect in weakness. Most gladly therefore will I rather glory in my infirmities, that the power of Christ may rest upon me. (II Corinthians 12:7-9)

Although the Apostle Paul gave the explanation of his

metaphor of the thorn in the flesh in the same line in which he mentioned this affliction, there has been a lot of confusion and controversy among those who would try to interpret the passage. As we saw in the Galatian passage, these demonic influences are associated with the results that take place in pour fleshly personality; however, when Paul spoke of his thorn in the flesh, many people get confused and fail to follow the logic that the real problem is demonic. The difficulties are based on several misconceptions which people hold in their minds when they read the scripture.

The first difficulty arises from the word "exalted." Many Bible scholars assume that the apostle is saying that there was a danger that he might get too proud because of the revelations he had received -- that he would become, as a mother might say of a little boy who was getting a little took cocky for his age, "too big for his britches." They think that Paul was suggesting that he might fall prey to the same trap about which he warned the Corinthians in his first letter to them: being puffed up through knowledge. (I Corinthians 8:1) In answer to this question, we must remember that our heavenly Father is the giver of all good and perfect gifts (James 1:17), that He is a perfectly wise God (Romans 16:27, I Timothy 1:17, Jude 1:25), and that the blessings He gives us add no sorrow with them (Proverbs 10:22). Let's stop and think about things on a natural level for just a minute: would any wise parent who has the well-being of his child in mind give him a pocket knife before he learned the Boy Scout rules about how to hold the knife and the stick while whittling? If we, as humans, are smart enough to know how to pick age-appropriate gifts for our children and only give them gifts when they are old enough to handle them, isn't it much more true about our Heavenly Father who is perfect in wisdom. It would seem that there must be something else implied in the term "exalted" in this passage; however, we must first move to another issue before we can fully gasp what this word must be intended to communicate.

The second misconception centers on the source of Paul's thorn. Many scholars assume that it was God who put this thorn into Paul's life. However, we need to step back from the passage a bit and look at it in a broader scope to get a clear understanding. Consider the logic -- or rather, lack of logic -- in the assumption that God gave Paul this thorn. If God knows that the revelations He is giving Paul are possible sources for him to fall into error, certainly He would not correct the situation by inflicting some sort of difficulties. Although we do find many examples in the Old Testament of when God brought calamity upon His people as judgment and correction when they were in rebellion and idolatry, there is no biblical precedent for God's having put bad things in His people's lives as a preventative. God's pattern for preventing His people from going astray is through the written word, His messengers such as prophets, and the personal direction of the Holy Ghost. Paul, as a mature believer and leader in the Body of Christ, would certainly have been able to have heard and followed the voice of God without some sort of painful thorn being inflicted in his life. The whole idea that God placed the thorn in Paul's life is against the very nature of God as the giver of good gifts. It also contradicts the pattern by which He leads His children.

The next thing we must consider in determining the source of Paul's thorn is the text itself. Paul clearly told us that it was a messenger of Satan. Since it was Satan's messenger, why should we assume that it was sent by God? In order to answer this question, some Bible students have turned to a couple passages from the Old Testament (I Kings 22 and II Chronicles 18) where a lying spirit was sent to deceive King Ahab of the Israel and King Jehoshaphat of Judah. However, careful examination of these incidents will reveal that these kings had already resisted the counsel and direction God had tried to give them; therefore, they -- unlike Paul who was receiving and living by the revelations God had given him -- were living in sin and rebellion. Furthermore, it must be noted that the lying spirit actually asked God's permission to go and deceive the kings. Therefore, it was not a case of God's having sent the evil spirit; rather, it was a case of His permitting it go. A very similar scenario is played out in the life of King Saul in I Samuel 16:14. Since Paul's case does not parallel the cases of these rebellious kings of the Old Testament, we have no reason to try to equate the passages. The simplest way to interpret this passage is to read it as it is written -- that Satan inflicted this thorn.

Having addressed the issue of the originator of the thorn, now we can go back the first question as to why it was sent. Seeing Satan as the originator of the thorn makes it readily obvious: it was sent to keep Paul from being exalted -- or brought to a place of prominence in the church and world -- because the Satanic kingdom suffered great losses every time Paul preached on the revelations he had been given. Even until today, the truths Paul brought to the Body of Christ are some of the most liberating principles ever taught. The devil desperately wanted to silence Paul. If he could keep people from receiving the apostle's message, he could keep them in his clutches! This thorn was not God's way of protecting Paul from pride, but Satan's way of trying to prevent Paul from gaining a place of advantage in his assault against the kingdom of darkness.

One other thing to remember when contemplating Paul's thorn would be that Paul has specifically addressed the issue of those in the Body who begin to feel self-important and inflated. In Romans 12:3, he warned them not to think more highly of themselves than they ought to think. If, in deed, Paul knew that this sort of self-exaltation would result in receiving a thorn in the flesh, isn't it likely that he would have incorporated a warning about such a result in this admonition about our personal evaluations of ourselves.

The next issue to consider would be the determination of the exact nature of Paul's thorn. Many teachers have proposed the notion that it was actually an eye disease. They, of course, draw upon the fact that Paul was blinded for three days at the time of his conversion on the road to Damascus. Added to this is Galatians 4:15 that we interpret to mean that he was having some sort of eye problem when he first preached in this city. However, such interpretation ignores the fact that Paul was healed of the blindness when Ananias laid hands on him and the fact that the Galatians passage does not specifically mention eye disease or blindness. Any conclusions drawn from this verse are based totally upon inferences and implications, not on specific factual information. However, we do have a direct information and explanation concerning the nature of this thorn given in the text itself.

Paul says that his thorn was a messenger from Satan. The English term "messenger" is translated from the Greek word *aggelos* that can also be translated "angel." Paul recognized that his thorn was one of Satan's angels (Matthew 25:41, Revelation 12:9) that we know as demons. His thorn was not a physical ailment at all, but a demonic attack upon his person in general and his ministry in specific. It was Satan's attempt to keep him from be established in a place "above measure," or above the capacity of the devil's forces. By simply reading the story of Paul's life, we can easily see that he was harassed on every side by zealous Jewish opponents who considered him a heretic and wanted to stop his evangelistic work, by jealous Christians who mistrusted him or thought that his acceptance of the gentiles without their having to abide by the Jewish law was in violation of the faith, and even by the tempestuous forces of nature. In a passage in the preceding chapter Paul spoke -- as he does in the passage we are studying -- of the infirmities in which he is determined to glory. In this section, he gave a compilation of these obstacles that have been thrown across his path as he ventured out to advance the kingdom.

Are they ministers of Christ? (I speak as a

fool) I am more; in labours more abundant, in stripes above measure, in prisons more frequent, in deaths oft. Of the Jews five times received I forty stripes save one. Thrice was I beaten with rods, once was I stoned, thrice I suffered shipwreck, a night and a day I have been in the deep; In journeyings often, in perils of waters, in perils of robbers, in perils by mine own countrymen, in perils by the heathen, in perils in the city, in perils in the wilderness, in perils in the sea, in perils among false brethren; In weariness and painfulness, in watchings often, in hunger and thirst, in fastings often, in cold and nakedness. Beside those things that are without, that which cometh upon me daily, the care of all the churches. (II Corinthians 11:23-28)

This dark cloud that seemed to be following Paul around was actually a demonic force that manifested itself through various avenues -- sometimes through the forces of nature, sometimes through the Jewish religious leaders, and sometimes even through Paul's Christian brothers.

When Paul asked the Lord to remove this demonic attack, the heavens were silent on his first two requests. On the third approach, Lord answered that the grace that Paul had already been given was sufficient for him to deal with the attack himself. God said that He didn't need to intervene because He had already made provision for Paul to deal with his adversary. The same is true in all our lives; if we know the weapons that God has placed into our hands, we can become invincible in the face of any demonic attack!

One significant truth that we know about the devil is that he is a liar. (John 8:44) Not only is he a liar, the truth is not in him; therefore, it is impossible for him to tell the truth -- even if he wanted to. Even when he says something that really is the true, it comes out in a distorted manner. If it is true that he is a liar, then we have no reason to even listen -- much less believe him when he tries to tell us something.

Another thing that we know about the devil is that he is a slanderer. (Revelation 12:10) His very name, if we translate it directly from the Greek meaning, tells us that. A slander is an individual who says destructive things about another person. Maybe the things he says are outright lies, maybe they are exaggerations of the truth, maybe they are half-truths, or maybe they are the plain and simple truth but spoken in an inappropriate way or within a negative connotation.

Another fact concerning the devil is that he is a murderer and a destroyer (Revelation 9:11). Everything he does will eventually result in the death and destruction of those he influences. I think we have all heard the stories of the man who sold his soul to the devil; he was given great wealth and prestige for a few years, but eventually had to face eternal destruction. Maybe we don't such conscious pacts with the devil, but all who are involved with him wind up being killed by him. He may offer some alluring benefits for a time, but he will eventually demand his payment in the form of your very life. For some, the payment comes quickly in the form of debilitating drug dependencies, AIDS, alcoholism, bankruptcy, and premature death through suicide, violence, or disease.

Of course, the devil isn't omniipotent, omniscient, or omnipresent; so it is impossible for him to produce widespread havoc in the human family single-handedly. However, he has a massive entourage of assistants called demons who share explicitly in his evil and destructive nature. These creatures are not, as some suppose, the spirits of the dead come back to haunt the living. Rather they are the rebellious angels who were cast out of heaven along with their leader Lucifer (now known as Satan or the devil). This fact is very significant in that we can understand that they once knew the pleasures of heaven and once had fellowship with God Himself and once had free access the very person and nature of the Almighty. Having rejected this unspeakably beautiful relationship with divinity, they must have become totally depraved in their nature, mentality, and person in order to continue to exist in their rebellion. Therefore, it is natural that their character would demand such activities as listed in the Bible: kill, steal, destroy, lie, vex, torment, make blind, make deaf, make dumb, make epileptic, cause foaming at the mouth, cause convulsions, cause to seem as dead, cause to cut oneself, cause to be wild, cause to live in graveyards, cause to be naked, cause to be insane, give wrong doctrines, produce lust, oppress, and eventually possess.

The passage we have begun to study told us that Jesus dealt with human captivity, and we have learned that it is also our job to do the same. Therefore, it would be good to ask the question as to what are the areas in which humans can be taken into captivity. The answer is far-reaching. Perhaps the first area is in the thought life. Many people become captive to negative, erroneous, or limited thinking. I once had a friend whose dog was notorious for chasing cars. To remedy the problem, my friend chained the dog so that he couldn't get to the street. The first few times that a car came down the road, the dog charged after it and was thrown for a flip in the air when he suddenly came to the end of the chain. Eventually the dog recognized his limits and learned to stop before somersaulting at the end of the rope. Finally my friend removed the chain, but the dog had become so accustomed to his limitation that he never ran any further than the spot where he chain once terminated. He would bolt after a car with full steam and bark as fiercely as any savage dog on the planet, but he would suddenly screech to a halt at the imaginary boundary. His thinking overruled reality. So it is with those who are under demonic captivity; they cannot live in the truth and freedom of God because they are held by chains that exist only in their minds. These limits imposed by Satan and his messengers make these people think of failure rather than success; they make the subjects feel inferior rather than normal; they make the captive see the dark cloud and miss the silver lining.

Another area in which people are held captive is the physical arena where disease and addictions can partially or totally debilitate the one under attack. In addition to the physical realm, captivity can operate in a person's spiritual life producing such compulsions as lust, anger, and hatred. These actions or attitudes may be totally foreign to the normal nature of the individual; but because of the diabolic captivity, these compelling forces overrun the person's natural personality. The emotional arena can also become prisoner through worry and fear.

In Jesus' first sermon, He identified His ministry as operating in several areas, one of which was to preach deliverance to the captive. (Luke 4:18) His entire life demonstrated that He not only brought the message of deliverance to the captive but also He gave them the deliverance they needed.

Jesus left us with a promise -- or should I say "command" or maybe even "warning" or "threat" -- concerning our own ministries: we are to do the same works that He did and even greater works! (John 14:12) That means that we, too, are to preach -- and practice -- deliverance! I guess that it really depends on own personal faith and commitment levels whether we perceive such a statement as a promise, a command, a warning, or a threat!

Paul left us some simple instructions concerning this mission of deliverance upon which Jesus has directed us to embark.

> In meekness instructing those that oppose themselves; if God peradventure will give them repentance to the acknowledging of the truth; And that they may recover themselves out of the snare of the devil, who are taken captive by him at his will. (II

Timothy 2:25-26)

Here we learn that people who need deliverance are in the snare of the devil. Perhaps it would be good for us to review a few of the facts that we know about the devil as we begin to think about what he is doing.

In trying to understand how we can obtain deliverance by renewing the way we think, let's begin by remembering who the devil is and how he and his demons work in our lives. According to Jesus' words in John 10:10, the devil is a thief and he comes to kill, steal, and destroy. While God wants to bless us in every area of our lives, the devil and his demonic associates want to destroy us in each of these areas. If it is God's will that we prosper and be in health, even as our souls prosper (III John 2), then it is the devil's desire that we meet with financial ruin, suffer with poor health, and live in spiritual poverty. He desires to steal and destroy everything that God gives us until he is eventually able to take our very lives.

Let's take the area of finances as a simple example of how renewing our minds can bring us deliverance. It is God's will that we live in prosperity, but the devil desires to steal that prosperity from us; therefore, at any point we find ourselves in debt or financially strapped, we can say that we are demonized because we are under the influence of the devil who has been stealing God's intended blessing from us. Of course, there are always a variety of reasons why a person may get into debt: accidents, sicknesses, layoffs, and other unforeseen emergencies. However, the main reason that most of us find ourselves in financial trouble is because we are conformed to this world -- we think like the rest of the world tells us to think. A wardrobe that is still perfectly good must be replaced because the new styles for the season are out and our clothes are now out of fashion. A designer came up with a new look, an advertising agency put it on TV and in magazines, and a marketing expert displayed it in the local store -- and even though we had to purchase it with money we don't really have, we rushed out like the rest of the secular world to get it. Being conformed to this world's thinking brought us under the demonic control of debt. In the arena of our finances, we are demonized! However, as we begin to renew our minds to think like the kingdom of God rather than the kingdom of this world, we realize that we don't need to "keep up with the Joneses" because our self-esteem is determined, not by what others think of us, but by what God thinks of us. As we renew our minds by reading and meditating upon the Word of God, we learn that we are accepted in the beloved even if our clothes are last year's styles. As we continue to change our attitudes about ourselves and our possessions, our buying habits will change and our bills will be reduced. The result is that we are less and less under the bondage of debt -- less and less demonized!

Apply this same scenario to every area of your life -- health, morals, relationships, and attitudes -- and imagine how dramatically your life can be transformed. The end result of your deliverance will be that rather than living under the control of the devil's bad, unacceptable, and imperfect will, your life will demonstrate the good, acceptable, and perfect will of God.

Of course, we all are just like Paul in hoping for a once-for-all deliverance from the thorns in our flesh. Such spectacular divine interventions certainly can and do occur. However, the full story is usually not quite over with the "amen" at the end of the deliverance prayer. Although talking about a physical liberation rather than a deliverance from demonic influence, Paul addressed the issue of once-for-all deliverance versus ongoing deliverance in II Corinthians 1:10 when he says, "Who delivered us from so great a death, and doth deliver: in whom we trust that he will yet deliver us." While speaking of past deliverance in a once-for-all, instantaneous sense, he speaks of the present deliverance as ongoing and progressive. The deliverance yet to come is referred to as a final and complete act. It is possible to receive a dramatic deliverance from a spiritual oppression, but it is most likely going to be followed by a progressive work of renewal until we receive that ultimate deliverance when we give up our residence in Satan's territory by passing from this life through death or rapture or until the tempter himself is bound and cast into the bottomless pit and eventually in the lake of fire. (Revelation 20:3, 10)

One final note should be emphasized above anything else in this study: it is not God's plan and it is never His will that we be subject to the devil's captivity.

> The thief cometh not, but for to steal, and to kill, and to destroy: I am come that they might have life, and that they might have it more abundantly. (John 10:10)
>
> For this purpose the Son of God was manifested, that he might destroy the works of the devil. (1 John 3:8)
>
> He that is begotten of God keepeth himself, and that wicked one toucheth him not. (1 John 5:18)
>
> Now thanks be unto God, which always causeth us to triumph in Christ, and maketh manifest the savour of his knowledge by us in every place. (II Corinthians 2:14)

Destroying the Works of the Devil

> He that committeth sin is of the devil; for the
> devil sinneth from the beginning. For this
> purpose the Son of God was manifested,
> that he might destroy the works of the devil.
> (I John 3:8)

The purpose of our being renewed people who function in the power and authority of Christ and are arrayed in the armor of God is so that we can destroy the works of the devil. When you destroy something, you totally obliterate it and move it out of the way. God did not manifest His Son for the purpose of having the devil and God stand side by side. He came to destroy the works of the devil. God's work in us is to totally remove and wipe out the works of the devil in us.

> Therefore if any man be in Christ, he is a
> new creature: old things are passed away;
> behold, all things are become new. (II
> Corinthians 5:17)

The Greek terminology used by Paul here indicates that we are new creatures in reference to quality; we are not new creatures in reference to time. To illustrate the difference between the two Greek words for "new," let's take an imaginary bicycle ride from my former home in Indiana to my present home in Colorado—a trip of around fifteen hundred miles. The bike I owned when I lived in Indiana was one step short of an antique; I bought it used in the early 1980s, so there is no way to guess just how old this relic really was. It did not have any gears to shift for easier peddling; its tires were not the slender, friction-efficient ones used on modern bikes; it was a plain, old-timey, one-speed bike that had been spray-painted yellow. Because of its color and vintage, my wife nicknamed it "The Yellow Submarine" after an old Beatles' song. Imagine that bright and early one morning I start out on my antiquated yellow bicycle. By the end of the day, I have collapsed on the side of the road when a kindly Good Samaritan stops by to see what the matter is. After I tell him my plan to peddle to the Rockies, he responds that I'll never make it on "that old bike." After a night's rest, I'm alive with the revelation that I must do something about "that old bike," so I peddle to the closest sporting goods store parking lot, circle behind the building and heave "The Yellow Submarine" into the dumpster. Then I walk inside and purchase the newest, sleekest, most efficient bicycle on the market and set out again for my destination some fifteen hundred miles ahead. By the end of this second day, I find myself again exhausted on the side of the road. When another Good Samaritan stops to inquire about my condition, I repeat to him the story of my proposed bicycle journey. His response is the same as last night's helper -- that I'll never make it on "that old bike." When I protest that this is not an old bike, that it has only been on the asphalt this one day, and that it is the latest in bicycle technology; he reiterates that I'll never make it on "that old bike" and drives away. Finally, I realize that my problem is not that my bike is old in terms of time -- it's old in terms of the quality of transportation. To get to Colorado, I need some updated form of transportation: an automobile or, better yet, an airplane. When we are in Christ, we are new creatures -- as radically different from our old man as a jet airplane is from my old "Yellow Submarine."

The purpose of God's coming into this world was not so that we could have a little bit of devil in us and a little bit of God in us at the same time. He came so that He could destroy the works of the devil -- totally eradicate them so that the only thing that will be in our lives is the work of God -- the new creatures we have become.

He came to destroy the works of the devil not only in us, but also in our families. When the Philippian jailer in Acts chapter sixteen asked Paul, "What must I do to be saved." Paul answered, "If you will believe then you and your whole household will be saved." Jesus did not come into this world so that we can have one Christian in a family of pagans. He came to destroy and annihilate the work of the devil in us and our families. Paul's message to the Philippian jailer was the same thing that the Apostle Peter announced on the Day of Pentecost, "This is for you and your whole family." (Acts 2:39)

The Son of God was manifest that He might destroy the works of the devil in our whole community. In Acts chapter nineteen, we read the story of how the people in Ephesus were so responsive to Paul's preaching that Demetrius the silversmith became irate because his business drastically fell off. There weren't enough pagans left to keep him rolling in riches. He called together all the other idol makers in the city to join with him against this move of God. The Temple of Diana was one of the seven wonders of the ancient world. The largest physical structure in Asia at the time, it was a magnificent piece of architecture. People came from around the world to worship there; but when Paul came to town, so many people converted to Christianity that the temple began to fall into neglect because there weren't enough pagans left to buy the images and give offerings. When Demetrius rose up to incite a riot against Paul, it was proof that the works of the devil were being destroyed -- not just in Paul's life, not just in Paul's family, but in the whole community. Jesus came for the purpose of destroying and defusing the works of the enemy in us, in our families, and our communities.

Acts 17:6 records the words of the angry Jewish mob who attacked Paul and Silas in Thessalonica, "These that have turned the world upside down are come hither also." This statement attests to the facts that Paul's ministry was not just a little local event and that Paul was not a man of just some local notoriety. When the work of the Son of God was manifest through Paul, it was destroying the work of the enemy worldwide. He and his partners were accused of turning the whole world upside down. The purpose of the gospel is to destroy the works of the enemy in us, in our families, in our communities, and in the whole world!

There is coming a time when this work will be finalized and the Son of God will be manifest in destroying the works of the devil in the whole world. Revelation chapter nineteen tells us that at that time He will appear on a white horse and we will be seated on a myriad of white horses behind him. Upon his thigh will be written, "The Faithful and the True One." (verse 11) And when He, in faithfulness and truth, confronts the devil head on, He will be able to destroy the works of the enemy in the whole world, Satan will be bound, and Death and Hell will be cast into the lake of fire. What a glorious consummation to the struggle that is going on now!

Before He can destroy the works of the enemy universally, and before He can destroy the works of the enemy in our community, and before He can destroy the works of the enemy in our family, Jesus must destroy the works of the enemy in us individually. That is the starting point. I personally believe that when we see that the works of the enemy are not being destroyed in the world or in our community or in our family, it is probably because they have not all been destroyed the way they should have been in us. God wants our lives at the point that He is totally Lord of all. He wants to totally rule and destroy all of the works of the enemy in our lives. When that happens, we can begin to see the ripple effect moving into our family, through our community, and into the entire world.

John 10:10 tells us that the thief comes to kill, to steal, and to destroy. But what is it that the devil wants to steal? Our money(?) Our health(?) Our hope(?) Our joy(?) Yes, he wants to steal all these -- and much, much more. He wants to steal all those things because they are of value to us. He wants to kill our bodies, our souls, and our spirits. He wants to destroy everything that we have built -- in the physical and in the spiritual. All that the devil wants to do is to kill, steal, and destroy -- in our lives, in our families, in our communities, and in the world. He will use every means that he can -- sickness, sin, war, natural disaster, evil rulers, crime, drugs, etc. If he has a tool, he will use it for his one purpose -- to kill, steal, and destroy.

But that same verse of John 10:10 says that Jesus came to bring life and life more abundantly. When Jesus gives us life, it is not just existence -- barely getting by -- it is life that is abundant! He wants us to enjoy living. One day we will live in heaven, but there is a whole lot of heaven to enjoy here on earth before we get to heaven. He wants us to experience heaven on earth in our process of getting to heaven. He has promised us that we could have joy (John 15:11), hope (I Corinthians 13:13), peace (John 14:26), health (Proverbs 3:8), prosperity (III John 2), salvation for our family (Acts 16:31), a safe community (Ezekiel 34:27) -- and the list goes on and on. He has promised that we could have favor with God and with man. (Proverbs 3:4) He has even promised that we could have friends (Proverbs 16:7), and love (I John 2:5), and freedom from fear (Psalm 91:5) and anger (Hosea 14:4). He has come to destroy the works of the enemy, and He wants us to have an abundant life in the place of everything negative that He has destroyed. However, many believers find themselves most of the time in the struggle between what God wants to do and what the devil wants to do because they have not learned how to release the destructive force of God upon the works of the enemy and then release the life-giving forces of God into their situations.

Scripture tells us that Job was a righteous and upright man. In fact, Job 1:1, 1:8, and 2:3 go so far as to call him perfect. From that evaluation, I would say that he had more going for him than most of us; however, the devil certainly had a great chance to do some destructive work in his life. Satan appeared before God one day and said, "Jehovah, I have been up and down in the world seeking what I can devour." God answered, "Did you happen to bump into my friend Job while you were down there?" "Well, not exactly," Satan replied, "I got near him, but I didn't actually bump into him, so to speak, because there was a hedge between him and me. I could peek over the hedge -- and, when I did, I saw that inside the hedge he had hundreds of camels, thousands of sheep, and billions of dollars. I couldn't get to him, but I recognized that he was there." God said, "I would like you to consider him. He is a prize to Me and an example of the fact that I want to give life and to give life more abundantly. He is my showpiece because he has tapped into what I want to give." "Ah, so what?" Satan retorted, "He is only yours because of everything you give him. If he didn't have all those things, he would be just as wicked and evil as the next guy." God's response was surprising, "We can test that. I give you permission to take his goods." You know the story of how the devil sent a wind that blew down the house and killed his sons and his daughters. Fire from the sky came down and burned up his livestock. Marauding invaders came in and took the rest of his possessions until he was left in poverty. Then God challenged the devil again, "Well, Job doesn't have all those goods anymore, but he is still doing well. He hasn't cursed me or betrayed me." The devil snapped back, "Well, that's because you still are holding on to him. If he didn't have his physical health, he would be mine." God confidently replied, "Okay, but just don't kill him. The power over his body is in your hand, but not the power over his life is not in your hand." So the devil afflicted Job with disease. He was ravaged from head to toe with sores and boils. There was no medical cure, but Job didn't have money to buy medical treatment even if it had been available. He wound up on a pile of ashes because ashes were soft and contained alkali that helped to somewhat relieve the infection. He was licked by dogs. He was in a pathetic situation. The only thing that was left in his life was the one thing he probably didn't need -- a wife, who advised him, "Why don't you just curse God and die." Then the devil sent four of Job's friends to him who just stood there and gazed at him. After a week of gazing, they finally decided to accuse. They picked his life apart trying to prove that he was the guilty one and that whatever was happening in his life was because of his sin. This went on for thirty-eight chapters as they rattled on, revealing their ignorance, point after point trying to bring Job into condemnation. Job refused condemnation. Finally, Job stood up and told those men, "I trust my God. And even if He kills me, I am still going to trust him." Job didn't understand the cosmic battle he was in. He never knew that he had to rebuke Satan. Therefore, the enemy was killing, stealing, and destroying in his life. The devil was doing exactly what he knows how to do -- and what he wants to do in your life and mine. But the key to the story is that Job kept clinging to God. When Job said to God, "I trust you," Satan knew that God had proven His point that Job was an upright man. Then God turned Job's captivity, demonstrating that it is His intent for us to have life and life more abundantly. He poured out upon Job double of everything that he ever had before. Even though Job didn't know any strategies of spiritual warfare, he clung to God and refused to lose his faith or be shaken in his relationship with God. Because he wasn't shaken, God then stepped in and fought his battle for him. He told the devil, "Enough is enough. Move out of the way." Then God went back to doing what He knows how to do -- giving life and giving abundant life.

In our lives, we have an advantage that Job didn't have. We understand who the devil is and what his plan is. God has given us the entire scripture. The book of Job was written long before Moses penned the book of Genesis. There was no written revelation for Job. There was no book for him to study in order to understand the revelation of the struggle of the ages. Today, we have the written Word so that we can understand the techniques and the tactics of the devil. The scripture tells us that we are not to be ignorant of the devil's devices. (II Corinthians 2:11) We have a revelation that we can use when we come into spiritual conflict. We can recognize the work of the devil and the work of God and can tap into God's provisions. We can believe for God to fight our battles for us, and we can join with Him in spiritual warfare as we hasten our victory. Job clung onto God, and God fought his battle for him. But we have the advantage of being able to actually join in that battle to precipitate a quick and a mighty victory. God intends to destroy the works of the enemy in our lives, the lives of our families, our communities, and our world -- and He has invited us to join Him in bringing about that victory.

Let's take a quick look at an interesting passage in the book of Acts, "God anointed Jesus of Nazareth with the Holy Ghost and with power and he went about doing good and healing all that were oppressed of the devil for God was with Him." (verse 10:38) Notice that the entire Trinity is mentioned in this verse: the Father, the Son and the Holy Spirit. They are working together for the purpose of doing good and to heal all who are oppressed by the devil. They have joined together in one dynamic trio to destroy the work of the devil. If the devil is at work, the Father, Son, and Holy Spirit have linked their unity together to come and destroy that work.

Our part is in James 4:7-8, "Submit yourselves therefore to God, resist the devil and he will flee from you. Draw nigh to God and he will draw nigh to you. Cleanse your hands you sinners, purify your hearts ye double minded." We have a three-part action: (1) submit ourselves to God; (2) resist the devil; and (3) draw nigh to God. In this three-part operation, two parts are toward God while only one is toward the devil. In the story of Job, we can see the power of the two parts that are directed toward God. Even though he submitted himself to God and drew near to God, he apparently wasn't even aware that there was a devil; therefore, he didn't even know that he was supposed to resist the devil -- much less how to do it! Because he refused to let his wife and so-called friends confuse him and mess with his mind, he eventually saw a victory. His victory was won totally by drawing near to God and submitting to Him. Image how much more might have happened in his life had he been able to add resisting the devil to his strategy! The powerful truth is that today we have all three elements available to us.

Notice one other thing about the passage from James. God calls for our total personality to be involved. "Cleanse your hands." If there is anything that we are physically involved with that is related to uncleanness -- stealing or adultery, for example -- we must wash our hands of it, and stop it. Then "purify your heart." This phrase addresses our soulical relationship. Romans 8:6 directs us, "For to be carnally minded is death; but to be spiritually minded is life and peace." The double-minded man sways back and forth between God and the devil, between his spirit man and his flesh. God tells us to purify our hearts and get rid of this double-mindedness which invalidates all that He would like to do in our lives. When we do that, we are able to resist the devil and see him flee from us because we have drawn nigh to God. Of course, the command to draw nigh to God and to submit our lives to Him is a directive toward our spiritual nature. God is at work in our lives to destroy the total work of the devil in us, our homes, our communities, and our world -- but it requires that we participate with His plan in our total personality: body, soul, and spirit.

While going through the temptations and trials of life, it is generally true that the darkest hour is just before the dawn. Just before daybreak is when it looks as though things are never going to work out. It is at this point that we must continue to remind ourselves not to give up and determine that we will never quit in resisting the devil and pressing into God. It was Jesus Himself who told us that it is the ones who endure all the way to end who will experience salvation. (Matthew 24:13, Mark 13:13)

The story is told of a gentleman in South Africa who owned a silver mine. He knew from the geological reports that there had to be silver in this area. By all indications, there had to be a bonanza of silver just waiting for him; but all he could find was rock -- no silver. He kept digging and digging until he finally decided to sell the mine. The first week that the new owner began digging inside that cavern -- where most of the manual labor had already been done by the previous owner -- he struck one of the most valuable veins of silver that had ever been found in Africa. He brought out millions of dollars in silver. The man who had done all the work gave up just one week too soon!

I remember a weekend retreat at a campground in the mountains of North Carolina. Although the campground was on the top of the mountain, the gate was at the bottom of the mountain. Some of the fellows who were joining us there for the camp got there late after the gate had been closed. They parked their car at the bottom of the mountain and started walking. They walked, and they walked, and they walked, and they climbed up toward the top of the mountain until they were too tired to go any further. Not knowing how much farther the campsite would be, they decided to walk back down the mountain and spent the night in their car. The next morning after the gate was unlocked, they drove on up the mountain and passed a landmark they recognized from the night before indicating the spot where they had given up and turned around. Around the next bend in the road was the campground. They could have had dinner with us, been in the evening meeting, enjoyed fellowship with all their friends around the warm fire, and slept in a nice warm cabin if they had turned one more corner. But they gave up too soon.

Second Kings chapter seven tells a story about four lepers. The enemy had surrounded the city of Samaria. The people inside the city were starving to death because the Syrians had cut off all supplies. They had depleted their supply of food, and all their rations were gone. The Bible tells us that women were even eating their own babies to keep themselves alive. These four lepers, living in the trenches in no-man's land between the Syrian army and the city wall, were outcasts left outside the city trying to forage for whatever food they could find. Eventually, they came to the point of being ready to give up because they knew that death was sure. Just then, one of them said to the others, "Why are we just sitting here until we die? Why don't we do something? If we sit here, we are going to die. If we go back to Samaria, we will surely die. Our only hope for possible survival is to go into the camp of the Syrians. Maybe they will have compassion and throw us some scraps." While they were on their way to the camp of the Syrians, God sent a noise, and the Syrians ran from the camp in fear for their lives. The lepers went into the camp and found enough food to literally "feed an army." They also found all their gold, silver, and all the other treasures that the Syrian army had collected in all their other campaigns up to that point. The lepers walked into untold wealth because one of them refused to give up. Not only were they blessed, but they brought deliverance to the city of Samaria. There was enough food for the entire city!

Joseph was a man who had every opportunity in life to give up. As soon as he had a dream of what God wanted to do in his life, his brothers became jealous, threw him in a pit, and sold him into slavery. God exalted him as the master of slaves over all of Potiphar's house to the point that Potiphar didn't even know how much money he had because he had left Joseph in control of it all. We all know the story of how Potiphar's wife tried to seduce Joseph and brought false charges against him when he resisted. Eventually, she had him thrown into prison where he met a man who promised to help him get released. However, the butler forgot about him, and Joseph had to spend two more years in the prison. Joseph could have -- no, by all natural means, should have -- given up. But when the Lord's timing was right, Pharaoh had a dream and the butler remembered Joseph. (Genesis 37:2-36, 39:1-41:57)

Jacob got himself into a lot of trouble: he stole his brother's birthright and cheated Esau out of his inheritance; he fled to Laban's house and finagled his uncle/father-in-law out of his possessions; he got himself into a place where he couldn't go back home because he knew that Esau was coming with a troop of men ready to kill him and Laban, with all of his forces, was pursuing him from the other direction; it was a dark hour in Jacob's life. There at Penuel (Genesis 32:28) -- in the middle between the two, being ground into powder emotionally and spiritually -- he turned to God, and God changed his name from Jacob (the supplanter) to Israel (the prince with God). Jacob's dark hour turned to dawn. A little later on in his life, Jacob had another experience in which he discovered that it was dawn just when all hope seemed to have been eclipsed. He loved his son Joseph, but Joseph was taken away from him. He had every physical reason to believe that Joseph was dead, but it seems possible that something inside of Jacob believed during all those years that there was a possibility that his beloved son might still be alive. I suspect that the old man must have somehow anticipated seeing his son again. When there were famine and starvation in the land, he had to send his sons to Egypt. But the news came back that his sons couldn't buy grain in Egypt without taking Benjamin with them -- a proposal that broke Jacob's heart because Benjamin was now his only hope of fulfilling the covenant promise that he had originally planned to pass on to Joseph. Poor Jacob was again pressed between the rock and the hard place -- he could not bear for Benjamin to leave his side; but if Benjamin did not go down to Egypt, all of his family would starve. Starvation was tearing him from one direction and the possible loss of Benjamin was tearing him from the other direction. This time, he was stretched and torn where before he had been pressed and ground. Just at that moment when it was the darkest hour; suddenly, the dawn came and he found that Joseph was indeed alive. Not only was he alive, he was Pharaoh's right-hand man in Egypt. Jacob was amazed that his son was already fulfilling the Abrahamic covenant of bringing blessing to the entire world -- even though that covenant had not even been passed to him yet! (Genesis 48:15-16)

The resurrection is the same. Our hope -- Jesus Christ,

the one we hoped would be the Redeemer -- had been beaten, assaulted, humiliated, crucified, and buried. But now He was missing! How much more desperate could the human race be? The only man we had any hope in has been so totally defiled and debased. He is dead, and now even His body had been stolen. But just when it was the very darkest hour, up from the grave He arose with a mighty triumph over His foes! The light shone, our dawn broke right at the moment when all hope was gone. Our darkest hour can be the birthing of our dawn.

I think I have only received one suicide note in my life. It came from one of my students who said that all hope was gone. He was flunking out of school. He was a failure. He was so far behind in his school debts that he would never get them paid. When I finally chased the guy down and talked with him, I had a lot of good news for him. His miracle was already in the mail, but the postman just hadn't delivered it yet. The day before, somebody had come in and paid off all his school bills, so he didn't owe the school one penny. He had a receipt coming in the mail, but he just hadn't read his mail yet. In his darkest hour, his dawning was already on the way. He thought that his grades were very low, but in fact he made the Dean's List that semester.

The father of one of my elementary school buddies had been a supply pilot during World War II. He would shuttle the planes to the front lines. He and five other supply pilots would fly six planes to the battle and then all get in one plane and fly back to the base. One evening they were all flying in formation over the Sahara Desert bringing planes to the troops in the European theater. All of a sudden, a sandstorm blinded them and they lost total visibility. They had to break formation and fly in opposite directions so they wouldn't crash into each other. The camel brigade and several search-and-rescue aircraft were sent out to try to find the missing pilots. One had crashed and died. The others were found either by local people or the French Foreign Legion. All were located except one who had landed in the middle of the desert. During the several days before they found him, he was exposed to the unrelenting heat of the desert and the unforgiving sun. With his water gone, he was beginning to die of dehydration. He came closer and closer to death, desperation, and insanity. Until finally, he said, "I give up," and he took his pistol and shot himself. The tragedy of the story is that the camel brigade was just over the dune ready to find him. In fact, they were close enough to hear the pistol shot. He gave up too soon.

We must determine to submit ourselves to God, resist the devil, and draw nigh to God -- and never give up! If we will apply these simple, but powerful, principles, we will see the works of the enemy destroyed in our personal lives, in our families, in our communities, and even to the ends of the earth! But this victory will not come without determination in the struggle.

The Violent Take the Kingdom by Force

In Matthew 11:12-15, Jesus said, "And from the days of John the Baptist until now the kingdom of heaven suffereth violence, and the violent take it by force. For all the prophets and the law prophesied until John. And if ye will receive it, this is Elias, which was for to come. He that hath ears to hear, let him hear." Luke records this same discourse, "The law and the prophets were until John: since that time the kingdom of God is preached, and every man presseth into it. And it is easier for heaven and earth to pass, than one tittle of the law to fail." (verses 16:16-17)

One of the most important principles to remember in trying to interpret scripture is that we have to treat it like a piece of real estate. When determining the value of a piece of land, there are three important factors to take into account: location, location, location. The same is true with the scripture; we must evaluate the passage in its context. The passages immediately before and after these verses about the kingdom of God deal with living under the Old Testament law. In fact, it is in this section where we find the oft quoted, "It is easier for heaven and earth to pass, than one tittle of the law to fail." (Luke 16:17)

The Greek word used in Luke sixteen for "violent" is *bias*. It is exactly the same word that is translated "take it by force" in Matthew. When Jesus said that violent men would press into God's kingdom, He was telling the people that a transition was coming from the period of the law to the age of grace. The dispensation of the authority of the law and the prophets came up to the time of John the Baptist who was spoken of as the final prophet to come just before the appearance of the messiah. (Matthew 11:10)

The Pharisees did everything they could to live by the law, and they reacted dramatically when they encountered anyone who did not join them in their diligence for the letter of the law. When John the Baptist came fasting, they accused him of having a demon because he didn't eat like them. But when Jesus ate with them and even turned water into wine, they called him demon possessed, a glutton, and a winebibber. (Matthew 11:18-19) They were happy with the *status quo* and wanted everything to stay the same under the authority of the Old Testament law. They had worked for fifteen hundred years to set up their legal traditions and sacred cows. They had in place all their intricate interpretations that allowed them to get around the regulations of the law that they could not meet. They were content; but, all of a sudden, there appeared a man who came to introduce a new generation that would shake and even remove their world. They resisted because they didn't want to lose their place and their authority under the law.

The word "violent" here means "by compulsion." It is used in the Greek to speak of a conscientious objector who was compelled by his government into military service when he doesn't want to fight and thinks that it is morally wrong to do so. The term is also used for sexual compulsion when a person loses control. *Bias* is also translated as "mighty" in Acts 2:2, "And suddenly there came a sound from heaven as of a rushing mighty wind, and it filled all the house where they were sitting." It was a wind of compulsion. The one hundred twenty believers in the Upper Room didn't make up their the languages they were speaking or select the words they were saying. Instead, there was an outside force like an invisible ocean wave that swept over them and compelled them to say things that they otherwise would not be able to vocalize.

In Matthew 12:24, we see how the Pharisees were pressing in on Jesus and accusing Him of violently taking away the kingdom of the law that they so preciously wanted to protect, "But when the Pharisees heard it, they said, This fellow doth not cast out devils, but by Beelzebub the prince of the devils." The violent legalist rose up to press against the kingdom of God as Jesus came to establish it. In Luke 11:17-21, we see Jesus' response,

> But he, knowing their thoughts, said unto them, Every kingdom divided against itself

is brought to desolation; and a house divided against a house falleth. If Satan also be divided against himself, how shall his kingdom stand? because ye say that I cast out devils through Beelzebub. And if I by Beelzebub cast out devils, by whom do your sons cast them out? therefore shall they be your judges. But if I with the finger of God cast out devils, no doubt the kingdom of God is come upon you. When a strong man armed keepeth his palace, his goods are in peace.

Jesus used the illustration of a strong man protecting his goods when a stronger one came in. Jesus, of course, is the stronger one. The stronger man overcame the strong man and took from him all his armor. The devil's armor is the authority (*exousia*) that he exerts through his lying deceptive words. The Bible teaches us that our activity is to be the stronger one and to rip off all the armor the devil is trusting in by destroying those thoughts which try to raise themselves above the knowledge of God. (II Corinthians 10:3-5) We rip off the devil's armor by speaking the truth. The stronger man then takes what the devil has stolen. The Greek word used here for "strong" and "stronger" is *iskuros* that means "having physical strength." Yes, the enemy has some physical strength; however, this passage says that we have more because we are stronger. As we have already learned, our strength is actually exceedingly great in comparison to his strength (Ephesians 1:19) -- we are not just a tad stronger, we are immeasurably stronger than our enemy. When the devil flings his lies, we can speak words of truth and demonstrate the fact that we are stronger.

Every time the kingdom of God is preached, there will be a violent force that will rise up against the power of the gospel. The world will compulsively -- beyond its own will -- turn against us and the kingdom of God. The attack is not against us personally. It is against the gospel that we preach. Those who rise up against us are not working in their own will; they are being compelled to do so. That is why we must remember Paul's warning that "we wrestle not with flesh and blood." Rather than taking offense personally, we must realize that our real enemy is the deception of the devil that is compelling those who oppose us. We can bind the strong man. We are stronger than the devil. We can take the goods he has stolen.

We bind the strong man by using the belt of truth, the gospel of peace, and the sword of the Spirit as weapons against the deceptive lies of the enemy. We can refute what he says by proclaiming the truth of the Word. That will bind up everything he says and his *exousia* is taken away. Because we have more strength, we can take his possessions.

Mark 3:29-30 reminds us, "But he that shall blaspheme against the Holy Ghost hath never forgiveness, but is in danger of eternal damnation: Because they said, He hath an unclean spirit." When the Pharisees called the work of the Holy Spirit the work of an unclean spirit, it was blasphemy against the Holy Spirit. They were learned men who knew the law. They knew the scriptures of the coming of the messiah. They should have been able to recognize the power of God in their day of visitation. They were not unlearned or ignorant men who, without calculation, had thrown off Jesus; they were in danger of blaspheming the Holy Spirit because they knew what they were doing and determined to do it anyway. When people have that violent compulsion to come against the kingdom of God, they are getting close to blaspheming the Holy Spirit -- a most serious thing because it is unforgivable. At that point, we have to recognize that our ability to step in and bind the strong man and pull off his armor and plunder his house is the thing that will determine their eternal destiny – whether they can ever get forgiveness or whether they will face eternal damnation. We have to step in, bind the strong man, and set the captives free. If we don't, they are very close to stepping across the line into an unforgivable situation. It is a matter of life and death -- not only for our own sakes, but also for the sake of those to whom we minister and even those who oppose us -- that we know how to use our armor and our weapons.

Warfare assumes tactics and implements. We don't go out to fight unless we have the proper implements. As Christians, we have a number of strategic implements and we need to learn to use them. Our first tactic is prayer. In Ephesians chapter six, Paul lists our armament: a belt of truth, a breastplate of righteousness, shoes of the gospel, a shield of faith, the helmet of salvation, and the sword of the spirit. These are all actually elements of protective armament, but Paul continues in Ephesians 6:18, "Praying always with all prayer and supplication in the spirit." Prayer is a weapon to help us in being able to move aggressively into spiritual warfare.

When Paul speaks of the sword of the spirit and then tells us to pray in the spirit, there is obviously a connection intended between the two. It is also clear that the sword, as an offensive weapon, could be used in aggressive, offensive prayer. Though we have already looked at this point previously, we need to make one simple observation before we see the full implications and impact of this concept. When Paul defines the sword of the spirit, he says that it is the Word of God, using a specific Greek term for "word." Of the two options available to him (*logos* and *rhema*), Paul chose the Greek term *rhema* that means a specific word as opposed to a general idea. In essence, what Paul was trying to communicate is that we need a specific word for every individual situation. We need to know which *rhema* to use when we are attacked physically. We have to know which *rhema* to use when we are attacked spiritually. We have to know which *rhema* to use when we are attacked financially. We need to know the individual Word to fire back at each situation. If the enemy is attacking with missiles, we need to use antimissile balistics specifically designed to destroying them. Ordinary rifles are good for one-on-one combat, but they cannot destroy an incoming missile. There is an individual weapon designed for each individual attack and we have to know our weapon of the Word of God to use in each situation. Paul doubly emphasizes the element of the Holy Spirit's involvement here when he says that the sword is the sword of the spirit and that the prayers must be in the spirit. To understand exactly what he is trying to say here, we must flip back to the book of Romans and see what he said there about praying under the direction of the Holy Spirit.

> Likewise the Spirit also helpeth our infirmities: for we know not what we should pray for as we ought: but the Spirit itself maketh intercession for us with groanings which cannot be uttered. And he that searcheth the hearts knoweth what is the mind of the Spirit, because he maketh intercession for the saints according to the will of God. And we know that all things work together for good to them that love God, to them who are the called according to his purpose. (verses 8:26-28)

The popular verse of Romans 8:28 about everything working together for our good cannot be separated from the verses that come before it. Verse twenty-eight begins with "and," a conjunction which means that there is something before it which has to be hooked together with it. In reading it in context, we see that the only time we can know that things will work together for good is when we have prayed in the Holy Spirit about our situations. We all have our own weaknesses and shortcomings, but the Holy Spirit overcomes them because He prays for us according to the will of God. You and I may not know how to pray for things because we don't know the full scope. We have a limitation to our knowledge, but the Holy Spirit isn't limited. He prays according to the will of God and He gives us exactly what we need to overcome the difficulty. It is at that point -- and only at that point -- that we can know that everything works together for good. In other words, the Holy Spirit will show us which one of the *rhema* truths of the Word of God applies to our immediate situation and then takes those *rhema* words and powerfully directs them to hit the targeted problem exactly on the bulls-eye every time.

We must know the power in the name of Jesus that will make every knee bow and every tongue confess. (Romans 14:11) And we also must know the power of the cross that is our redemptive force. Let's reread what Paul has stated as the most significant revelation we can have in order to lead a victorious Christian life.

> [I] cease not to give thanks for you, making mention of you in my prayers; That the God of our Lord Jesus Christ, the Father of glory, may give unto you the spirit of wisdom and revelation in the knowledge of him: The eyes of your understanding being enlightened; that ye may know what is the hope of his calling, and what the riches of the glory of his inheritance in the saints, And what is the exceeding greatness of his power to us-ward who believe, according to the working of his mighty power, Which he wrought in Christ, when he raised him from the dead, and set him at his own right hand in the heavenly places, Far above all principality, and power, and might, and dominion, and every name that is named, not only in this world, but also in that which is to come: And hath put all things under his feet, and gave him to be the head over all things to the church, Which is his body, the fulness of him that filleth all in all. (Ephesians 1:16-23)

We must also know the power of our position as

covenant partners with God. This was the force that made David the victor when he confronted Goliath. He looked at Goliath and saw the one thing that the others had not -- that Goliath was uncircumcised and, therefore, did not have a covenant with the God of the earth. (I Samuel 17:26) On the other hand, David saw that he could not be defeated and would have God's strength to do the job because of his own covenant rights. The sacraments that we receive in the church are confirmations of our covenant rights. When we receive communion, it is a reminder of our covenant right of healing and our redemption. "This is my body that is broken for you. This is my blood which is a new covenant." (I Corinthians 11:24-25) We have spiritual authority though the communion. Through it, we are reminded, encouraged, and energized with our covenant right. There is covenant power that occurs in the communion if we know how to recognize and appropriate it. Paul said that there were many who were sick and had died prematurely because they took the communion unworthily -- without understanding what it was all about. (I Corinthians 11:27) The Lord implemented baptism for us to have a covenant reality in our lives. When a new convert goes down under the water and is brought back up again, it is a confirmation that he has died to sin and is now raised to life. According to Romans chapter six, baptism is a point of reference from which we can call our covenant rights into being and we can point to as a confirmation that the old man has died and the new creation now lives. Colossians 2:12-14 also emphasizes that we are raised with Him because of the faith that we release through that event. If we go through water baptism as a ritual without placing our faith into what God has done for us, it is just a religious exercise and has no more spiritual power than just getting wet. But if we recognize it as such, baptism can become a powerful weapon against the enemy when he tries to accuse us of still living in our old sins.

Music is one of the powerful forces that we can use as a

weapon against the enemy. It has been said that the army marches by its music. I remember the story of a man who went to fight in World War II. He heard a marching band playing at the recruiting office and got so caught up in the music that he enlisted on the spot; he actually went off to fight because of the music. No football team goes to the gridiron without having a fight song. There is something about patriotic music that gets inside of us and moves us to go to fight. Music also brings us into unity. On Sunday mornings when we all come in from our busy weeks, we are all moving in a multitude of different directions. But when we begin to sing, we all have our minds set on the same words, we all have our voices singing the same note, and we all have our spirits on the same truth. When we start to sing, it brings us into unity. Even though there may be a lot of division and contention among the members; but in singing, the church comes into unity and God begins to manifest.

Remember what we have learned from the story of Jehoshaphat -- when the enemy heard the singers coming, they became so confused that they fought one another. When Israel came in, all they had to do was to pick up the spoils of war. We can battle with our praise. David calmed the evil spirit that was in Saul when he played his harp. (I Samuel 16:23) Paul admonishes us to sing to ourselves, "Speaking to yourselves in psalms and hymns and spiritual songs, singing and making melody in your heart to the Lord." (Ephesians 5:19) Music can set a victorious atmosphere in our homes. There is a spiritual force that rises up inside us through music.

We have the gifts of the Holy Spirit operating in our lives as strategic spiritual implements. When the king of Syria had declared war against the land of Israel, he called his cabinet together to secretly plan out his next strategy of attack. But through a word of knowledge, God would speak the enemy's plans to the prophet Elisha who would then tell the king of Israel how to avoid the enemy's next line of attack. (II Kings 6:8-12) Through the gifts of the Spirit, we can do exactly the same thing in our spiritual warfare. As we have learned in a previous section, everything in our lives may not naturally work out for our best. We may lose a few battles. But when we begin to pray in the Holy Spirit about our challenges, we have the same advantage that Elisha gave to the king of Israel. We have the spiritual gifts as supernatural weapons that overcome the enemy's tactics against us.

Our tithes and our offerings can be tactics that we can use against the enemy. Haggai tells the story about the people of Israel after they came back from the Babylonian captivity. They had started building the temple, but then started building their own houses and their own businesses. The temple project was left half-finished. God sent Haggai to ask the people why it was that even though they worked hard all day long and earned money, their money seemed to slip through their fingers and they could never get ends to meet. It was like putting their money in bags with holes in them. Take a look around, and you'll immediately recognize that most people today live exactly like that. Every time they think that they are just about to make the ends meet, someone moves the first end! They are always a day late and a dollar short. Haggai told the people of Israel that their problem was that they had not completed the job they were sent to Jerusalem to do -- to rebuild the temple. From the very minute that the people made the decision to put their own affairs aside and complete the temple, their situation turned around one hundred and eighty degrees. "Is the seed still in the barn? As yet the vine, the fig tree, the pomegranate, the olive tree has not yielded their fruit: but from this day I will bless you." (Haggai 2:19) The prophet Malachi made this experience into a universal principle that will work in all our lives when he penned the promise of God that He would rebuke the devourer for our sake in the day that we decide to bring the full tithes and offerings into the storehouse. (Malachi 3:10-11) Until we use this tactic of our giving, we cannot pull ourselves out of the battlefield of finances. If we are halfhearted or untrue in our tithes and offerings, we will always be in the devil's battlefield. But we will push beyond his battlefield. If we can give our tithes and offerings, we will be blessed and the devourer will be rebuked.

Of course the most important tactics of our warfare is our right thinking. In Romans 12:2, Paul taught us to renew our minds. In Philippians 4:8, he gave us some sound advise on how to go about that renewal process by telling us to meditate only on things that are true, honest, just, pure, lovely, of good report, virtuous, and praiseworthy.

But one significant element still remains to be considered. All these tactics are like arrows, but we need a bow to make them effective. The bow that the Lord places in our hand is faith. We can't just give; we must give in faith. We can't just sing; we have to sing in faith. We can't just quote scriptures; we have to do it in faith. Faith is like the bow that we can pull back to propel those arrows.

Warfare also assumes the presence of a soldier. Second Timothy 2:3 calls us good soldiers. We have to be soldiers in uniform. Ephesians 4:22-24 and Colossians 3:8-14 tell us about getting properly attired for our Christian life by putting off the old man and putting on the new man -- putting on our spiritual cloak so that we are then able to put on the armor of God on top of it. (Ephesians 6:11, 13) We could further this study by examining Colossians 3:8-17, Romans 13:12, James 1:21, and Hebrews 12:1 to get a better understanding of some of the things that we must put off in order to put on our uniform; however, a simple parallel from the natural area should serve the purpose. Just like it is impossible for a soldier to put his uniform on top of his jeans and sweatshirt or on top of his business suit, it is impossible for a Christian warrior to try to dress in the armor of God until he first removes the things that have identified him with his former life in this world.

We have to be in formation in the Body of Christ. (I

Corinthians 12:14) We have to recognize what our individual position is in the Body. Some are hands, some are feet, some are eyes, some are ears. In a physical army, each soldier has to recognize his specific position and fill that unique spot. There are those people who are on the frontline shooting the artillery. There are people behind the lines bringing up the supplies. There are the medics who take care of the injured along the way. Every person has his own position. Every person cannot be a supply officer or a frontline soldier or a medic. But it takes a certain number of each one -- and if any one of those integral elements is lacking, we won't have a full army functioning properly. In the Body of Christ, we have to know our positions, get in them, and fulfill our specific functions. "But unto every one of us is given grace according to the measure of the gift of Christ." (Ephesians 4:7)

An army is no good unless there is communication. Remember the constant theme that used to appear in the old war movies -- the dead batteries in the radio when the frontline soldiers are trying to contact the command post. This scenario is always a major catastrophe and turning point in the movie! In our spiritual lives, we have to be in communication so we are able to hear from and speak to the command post. There must be communication going on in the battlefield. If we don't hear our commanding officer through the leading of the Spirit, we are not in proper relationship and we won't be able to fight. The ability to communicate is definitely a turning point in our victory or defeat.

We have to be soldiers on readiness. Matthew chapter seventeen tells the story about a father who brought his child to the disciples to be healed of epilepsy, but the disciples could not cast the demon out. When Jesus came down from the Mount of Transfiguration, the father ran to Jesus and told him the whole story of how the disciples had not been able to cast the spirit out of the boy. We would anticipate our kind, loving, gentle, patient Jesus to be gracious with His disciples and coach them through the deliverance process again. But instead, He turned around and rebuked them for their unbelief and disobedience. I guess that He must have left His WWJD bracelet on the dresser that morning and didn't have it to remind Him how to be kind and sweet. Actually, He had a reason for scolding His disciples. In chapter ten, He had given them the power over all demons, but somewhere between chapters ten and seventeen, they had lost their authority. Jesus was scolding them, not because they couldn't cast out the spirit, but because they had lost the authority that He had already given them. He then added that the spirit would only come out through prayer and fasting. Apparently, the disciples had stopped praying and fasting between chapters ten and seventeen; therefore, they were not ready to deal with a demonic problem when it arose. A dramatic example of this lack of readiness in modern history can be found in the early Sunday morning attack on Pearl Harbor when the men on the naval base weren't ready. Only a minimal number of men were on duty. Many of the sailors had partied the night before and were still asleep. When they weren't ready, destruction came. Likewise, we as soldiers in the army of God many times get too lackadaisical and let down our guard, leaving ourselves unready when spiritual conflicts arise. We must learn to be ready because we can lose battles if we are attacked when we aren't being vigilant. (I Peter 5:8)

Warfare assumes choosing up sides. Remember choosing up sides to make up the ball teams when you were a kid. Joshua commanded the people of Israel that they would have to choose whose side they were going to be on -- the gods of the Egyptians, the gods of the Amorites, or Jehovah God. (Joshua 24:15) In the church today, some have become traitors; they wear the coat of one side but talk the talk of the other side. There are those who wear the robes of the church, but they are talking the talk and having the mindset of the enemy. If we are going to be in the warfare, we have to choose to be on one side or the other. We can't be conformed to the present world; rather, we must be transformed to the kingdom of God. (Romans 12:2)

Warfare assumes territories. There are territories that have been set with literal boundaries and principalities in place over them. We must decide which territory is whose, and we have to go in and take territory that God wants us to have. When we take a territory, we go in and pull down the flag and raise our flag in its place. We, as Christians, need to come into every area of our lives and the lives of those around us and tear down the enemy's stronghold and raise our flag.

Warfare assumes a purpose. The warfare we are talking about is not just a rivalry between the Hatfields and McCoys who carried on a family feud for many years without even understanding why it was that the two families were at odds. Our warfare has a real purpose. Reclaiming territory the devil is trying to take away from us is our purpose. Maintaining our covenant possessions is our purpose. We have an offensive purpose in reclaiming territory and a defensive purpose in maintaining what is ours.

Warfare assumes total involvement. Our spirits, our souls, and our bodies all have to be involved if we are going to win. We have already learned from James 4:7-8, "Submit yourselves therefore to God. Resist the devil, and he will flee from you. Draw nigh to God, and he will draw nigh to you. Cleanse your hands, ye sinners; and purify your hearts, ye double minded." We observed that our physical man was involved when we heeded the command to cleanse our hands, our soulical man was implicated when we purified our hearts, and our spiritual man was drawn in when we drew nigh to God and submitted ourselves to Him.

A Snake in the Grass -- or At Least in the Tree

Before we conclude our study, let's take one quick look at the first encounter that the human race had with our diabolical enemy. It's the familiar story of Satan's visit with Adam and Eve in the form of a serpent. (Genesis 3:1-6) When Paul analyzed the event in his epistles, he made a couple very revealing observations: in II Corinthians 11:3, he observed that Eve was beguiled through the serpent's subtlety; in I Timothy 2:14, he added that although Eve was deceived Adam was not deceived by the serpent's smooth talk. Apparently, Adam recognized what was going down and went along with the program even though he knew better. Because he willingly surrendered the dominion that God had originally placed in his care (Genesis 1:26, 28), Satan was able to begin exerting authority on our planet. It stands to reason that if it was Adam, a human being, who gave the devil power or authority to work in the earth, then Adam, the human, has the responsibility of retracting that authority. Jesus Christ -- as a human and the last Adam (I Corinthians 15:45) -- did just that; He undid what the first Adam messed up! But that's not the end of the story. He then left the continuing authority in the hands of other humans -- you and me! Let's go forth and occupy until He returns and inflicts the final blow on Satan and all his fiendish subjects!!

Epilogue

A Primer of Verses to Help Establish Your Place of Victory

A friend of mine had suffered from serious depression that totally immobilized him. He could not function at work, at home, or in any level of society. Spiritually, emotionally, physically -- his life had almost totally shut down. He had not only come to a standstill, he was rapidly losing ground through the loss of his marriage, his employment, and his finances. Soon, the downward spiral became a headlong plunge toward the abyss. When he called me for prayer, I typed out the following verses and asked him to read and repeat them until he was able to recite them by heart -- not just <u>by</u> heart, but <u>from</u> the heart. A few weeks later he called back with the victorious testimony that he had been miraculously set free. As we close this study, I'd like to leave these scriptures with you to help prime the pump for any spiritual conflict you may encounter.

<u>II Corinthians 2:14</u> Now thanks be unto God, which **always causeth us to triumph in Christ**, and maketh manifest the savour of his knowledge by us in every place.
<u>I John 4:4</u> Ye are of God, little children, and have overcome them: **because greater is he that is in you, than he that is in the world.**
<u>Luke 10:19</u> Behold, I give unto you power to tread on serpents and scorpions, and **over all the power of the enemy**: and nothing shall by any means hurt you.
<u>Romans 8:35-39</u> Who shall separate us from the love of Christ? shall tribulation, or distress, or persecution, or famine, or nakedness, or peril, or sword? As it is written, For thy sake we are killed all the day long; we are accounted as sheep for the slaughter. Nay, in all these things **we are more than conquerors through him that loved us**. For I am persuaded, that neither death, nor life, nor angels, nor principalities, nor powers, nor things present, nor things to come, Nor height, nor depth, nor any

other creature, shall be able to separate us from the love of God, which is in Christ Jesus our Lord.

Romans 16:20 And the God of peace shall bruise **Satan under your feet** shortly. The grace of our Lord Jesus Christ be with you. Amen.

Colossians 2:15 And having **spoiled principalities** and powers, he made a shew of them openly, triumphing over them in it.

Ephesians 1:19-21, 2:6 And what is the exceeding greatness of his power to us-ward who believe, according to the working of his mighty power, Which he wrought in **Christ**, when he raised him from the dead, and set him at his own right hand in the **heavenly places, Far above all principality, and power, and might, and dominion, and every name that is named,** not only in this world, but also in that which is to come: And hath raised us up together, **and made us sit together in heavenly places in Christ Jesus**:

Matthew 10:8 Heal the sick, cleanse the lepers, raise the dead, **cast out devils: freely ye have received**, freely give.

Mark 16:17 And these signs shall follow them that believe; **In my name shall they cast out devils**; they shall speak with new tongues;

Luke 10:18 And he said unto them, I beheld **Satan as lightning fall from heaven**.

I John 3:8 He that committeth sin is of the devil; for the devil sinneth from the beginning. For this purpose the **Son of God was manifested, that he might destroy the works of the devil**.

Dr. Delron Shirley is founder and president of Teach All Nations Mission, an evangelical educational ministry. He is also an adjunct faculty member at Charis Bible College in Colorado Springs and serves as a consultant for Every Home for Christ in their discipleship department. Before moving to Colorado, Delron served for twenty-five years as dean of World Harvest Bible College and Indiana Christian University and worked as a chaplain in Yosemite National Park.

The ministry of Teach All Nations Mission takes him and his wife throughout the world where they teach in conferences for national pastors and leaders. In addition to the ministry to the nationals, Delron and Peggy are strongly committed to inspiring others to go beyond their borders to share the Good News; thus, they lead several mission trips each year to introduce teams of students to live on the mission field.

As a tireless writer, Delron has published numerous books, many of which have been translated into the languages of the countries where he ministers.

Delron or Peggy Shirley can be contacted for ministry requests at: TEACH ALL NATIONS MISSION
3210 Cathedral Spires Dr.
Colorado Springs, CO 80904
719-685-9999
www.teachallnationsmission.com
teachallnations@msn.com

CPSIA information can be obtained
at www.ICGtesting.com
Printed in the USA
FSOW02n0140170817
37458FS